Oscillators

SIMPLIFIED
WITH
61 PROJECTS

DELTON T. HORN

No. 2875
$17.95

Oscillators
SIMPLIFIED
WITH
61 PROJECTS

DELTON T. HORN

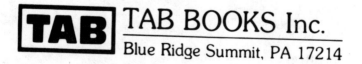

TAB BOOKS Inc.
Blue Ridge Summit, PA 17214

788-98

FIRST EDITION
FIRST PRINTING

Library of Congress Cataloging in Publication Data

Horn, Delton T.
    Oscillators simplified, with 61 projects.

    Includes index.
    1. Oscillators, Electric.   2. Electronic circuits.
I. Title.
TK7872.O7H67   1987   621.3815′33   87-13882
ISBN 0-8306-0375-1
ISBN 0-8306-2875-4 (pbk.)

Questions regarding the content of this book
should be addressed to:

    Reader Inquiry Branch
    Editorial Department
    TAB BOOKS Inc.
    P.O. Box 40
    Blue Ridge Summit, PA 17214

Contents

Introduction

ONE OF THE MOST BASIC OF ALL ELECTRONIC CIRCUITS IS THE oscillator, or signal generator. Virtually all electronics systems incorporate at least one such circuit.

While information on signal generators is not terribly hard to find, there has been no single source devoted to the oscillator until now.

This book tells you all you need to know about oscillator and signal generator circuits for almost any application. Over 60 practical projects are included. These circuits can be readily adapted to suit your individual requirements.

List of Projects

Oscillators and Signal Generators

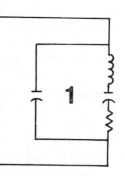

A T FIRST GLANCE, IT WOULD SEEM THAT THERE ARE AN IN-
finite number of electronic circuits. In a sense, there are. But
most complex circuits are actually made up of simpler sub-circuits.
For the most part, these simple sub-circuits consist of just a few
basic types: power supplies, amplifiers, filters, and oscillators.
These fundamental circuits are found time and again in electronic
circuitry.

This book closely examines the class of circuits known as
oscillators or signal generators.

WHAT IS AN OSCILLATOR?

In the simplest possible terms, oscillation is any repeating,
periodic effect. Some common physical examples are a swinging
pendulum, the back and forth motion of a spring, or the continual
back and forth motions of electrons in a conductor carrying
alternating current (ac).

In electronics work, an oscillator is a circuit that generates a
periodic (repeating) ac signal. Oscillation is always the result of the
periodic storage and release of energy. In the case of a pendulum,
energy is stored as the weight rises, and is released when weight
falls. In an electronic circuit built around an inductive-capacitive
network, energy is alternately transferred between the inductive
and capacitive reactances. An oscillator circuit can deliberately be
made to oscillate at a precise frequency.

Sometimes oscillation occurs even when it is not desired. This can happen in an amplifier circuit with too much gain, or a circuit which is improperly designed for the intended application.

There are many different types of oscillators. Most incorporate the feedback principle. These circuits consist of an amplifier with some of its output fed back, in phase, to the input.

A feedback oscillator requires some type of active amplifying device. This can be a transistor, a FET, a tube, an op amp, or a similar device. Since an active component is used, an external source of power is also needed. A resonant circuit is used to generate oscillations at a specific frequency. There are several types of resonant circuits, including inductive/capacitive networks, resistive/capacitive networks, and piezoelectric crystals, among others. In some circuits, specialized devices such as a Gunn diode or a Klystron tube is used to produce oscillation via negative resistance effects.

Some of the most important types of oscillator circuits are:

- ☐ The Armstrong oscillator
- ☐ The Colpitts oscillator
- ☐ The Hartley oscillator
- ☐ The Pierce oscillator
- ☐ The crystal oscillator
- ☐ The Gunn diode oscillator

WAVEFORMS

An oscillating or ac signal varies with time. If you draw a graph of the repeating pattern of the changing voltage over time, as shown in Fig. 1-1, you have drawn the waveform of the signal. Although an infinite variety of waveforms is theoretically possible, a few basic types are commonly generated with electron circuits.

The waveform illustrated in Fig. 1-1 is the most basic of all waveforms. It is called the sine wave, because it resemblances a graph of the trigonometric sine function. A sine wave consists of a single frequency component. The significance of this statement will become clearer shortly, when we discuss other waveforms.

This is a periodic waveform, like all oscillators produce. This means the waveform repeats the same pattern over and over. The number of times the pattern cycle is repeated in a second is the frequency of the signal. That is, if the pattern repeats for 855 complete cycles in a second, the signal has a frequency of 855 hertz (often abbreviated Hz).

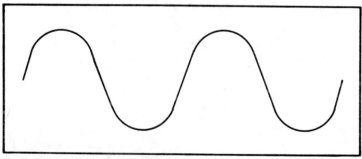

Fig. 1-1. The sine wave is the most basic waveform.

Metric prefixes are used for convenience to express higher frequencies. The two most common prefixes are kilo (k), which means thousand, and mega (M), which means million. That is:

$$MHz = 1000 \text{ kHz} = 1,000,000 \text{ Hz}$$

In older technical literature, frequencies are sometimes expressed in cps, or cycles per second; cps is identical to the hertz nomenclature, which is now standard.

$$1 \text{ cps} = 1 \text{ Hz}$$

(Strictly speaking, all oscillators generate sine waves. But other circuits, which are similar to oscillators, generate other, more complex waveforms, as explained in the next section of this chapter.)

In addition to the sine wave, there are several other common waveforms, each with its own special characteristics. Some of these are illustrated in Fig. 1-2. All non-sine waveforms are made up of multiple frequency components. The basic cycle repetition rate is still the main frequency of interest. This is called the fundamental frequency. Often this is the only frequency directly identified.

Additional waveforms that are whole number multiples of the fundamental frequency are also included in the make-up of the waveform. These higher frequency components are called overtones, or harmonics. Generally, the harmonics are weaker (at a lower amplitude) than the fundamental frequency component.

Which harmonics are present, along with their relative amplitudes and phase relationships, determine the composite waveform. Theoretically, any waveform can be synthesized by the correct combination of component sine waves.

3

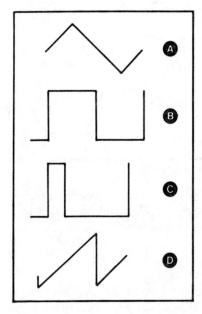

Fig. 1-2. Other common waveforms include the triangle wave (A), the square wave (B), the rectangle wave (C), and the sawtooth wave (D).

In many applications, complex waveforms are more desirable than sine waves. As it turns out, it is often simpler to generate certain complex waveforms directly, rather than synthesizing them from multiple sine waves.

Symmetrical waveforms contain only odd harmonics. That is:

$$3 \times \text{fundamental}$$
$$5 \times \text{fundamental}$$
$$7 \times \text{fundamental}$$
$$9 \times \text{fundamental}$$
$$11 \times \text{fundamental}$$

Even harmonics do not occur in symmetrical waveforms:

$$2 \times \text{fundamental}$$
$$4 \times \text{fundamental}$$
$$6 \times \text{fundamental}$$
$$8 \times \text{fundamental}$$
$$10 \times \text{fundamental}$$

Typical symmetrical waveforms are the triangle (or delta) wave (Fig. 1-2A) and the square wave (Fig. 1-2B). The names are derived from the appearance of the waveform graphs. Both triangle waves

4

and square waves contain all of the odd harmonics. The difference between these two waveforms is in the relative amplitude of the harmonics. All of the harmonics in a triangle wave have lower amplitudes than those of the square wave.

On other symmetrical waveforms, one or more of the odd harmonics may be missing. Since these waveforms are symmetrical, there are no even harmonics.

Non-symmetrical waveforms may contain either odd or even harmonics, or both. Typical nonsymmetrical waveforms include the rectangle, or pulse wave (Fig. 1-2C) and the sawtooth, or ramp wave (Fig. 1-2D). The harmonic waveform of a rectangle wave is determined by the ratio between the high level time to the total cycle time. This ratio is called the duty cycle of the pulse.

A square wave is actually a rectangle wave with duty cycle of 1:2. As mentioned earlier, it contains all of the odd harmonics, but none of the even harmonics. In other words, all of the harmonics which are multiplies of 2 are missing. Its harmonic make-up consists of frequency components at the following frequencies:

> Fundamental
> 3rd harmonic
> 5th harmonic
> 7th harmonic
> 9th harmonic
> 11th harmonic
> 13th harmonic
> and so forth

The higher the harmonic, the weaker it is. At some point, the amplitude of the harmonics becomes so low that they are no longer worth mentioning. This is true of most common waveforms.

In a rectangle wave with a duty cycle of 1:3, every third harmonic is missing. The harmonic make-up looks like this:

> Fundamental
> 2nd harmonic
> 4th harmonic
> 5th harmonic
> 7th harmonic
> 8th harmonic
> 10th harmonic
> 11th harmonic

13th harmonic
and so forth

Although both odd and even harmonics are included, any harmonic that is a multiple of 3 is not included.

If the duty cycle is 1:4, all harmonics, except those which are multiplies of 4, are included:

Fundamental
2nd harmonic
3rd harmonic
5th harmonic
6th harmonic
7th harmonic
9th harmonic
10th harmonic
11th harmonic
13th harmonic
and so forth

This pattern holds true for any duty cycle. Where the duty cycle is 1:X, any harmonic which is a multiple of X is absent from the waveform's make-up. All harmonics that are not multiplies of X are included in the waveform's make-up.

In a sawtooth waveform (Fig. 1-2D), all harmonics, both even and odd, are included. The ramp portion of the wave may be either ascending (slope from low to high) or descending (slope from high to low). The main difference between ascending and descending sawtooths is the phase relationship of the various frequency components of the waveform.

SIGNAL GENERATORS

To some extent, the terms oscillator and signal generator are interchangeable. Both oscillators and signal generators are circuits which produce ac (fluctuating) electrical signals. However, use of the term oscillator is frequently restricted to circuits which generate only sine waves.

Other ac waveforms are also commonly used for various applications. Oscillator-like circuits which produce other waveforms, instead of (or in addition to) sine waves, are usually called signal generators.

This distinction is somewhat arbitrary, but convenient. An oscillator generates sine waves. A signal generator generates one or more of the more complex waveforms. Because there is an important difference in the basic design of most oscillators and most signal generators, this book distinguishes between the two types of circuits on the basis of the signal produced.

RELAXATION OSCILLATORS

Most signal generator circuits fall into one of two basic categories:

- ☐ Relaxation oscillators
- ☐ Feedback oscillators

The main difference between the two is that all feedback oscillators are built around an active (amplifying) component, such as a transistor, a tube, or an op amp. Relaxation oscillators can be built around passive (non-amplifying) devices.

Feedback oscillators are discussed in the next section of this chapter. For now, let's concentrate on relaxation oscillators.

By the definition given above, a relaxation circuit is actually a signal generator rather than an oscillator because it does not produce a sine wave. Any of several non-sine waveshapes can be generated from a relaxation circuit, depending on the specific design. Typical relaxation waveforms include sawtooth waves and pulse waves. (A pulse wave is a very narrow rectangle wave.) Many textbooks define the relaxation oscillator as a circuit that automatically switches between two stable states. This definition is really most accurate for the multivibrator, a circuit which is closely related to the relaxation oscillator. (Multivibrators will be covered in later chapters of this book.)

Relaxation oscillators occur in nature. These natural oscillators provide a convenient way to understand the operation of an electronic relaxation circuit. Imagine a tree with a low-hanging branch that extends below the water level of a fast-moving stream. The motion of the water carries the end of the branch downstream. Because the branch is firmly attached to the tree, this motion increases the tension of the branch. At some point, the branch's tension is greater than the force of the waterflow. The branch then swings back to its original relaxed position, and the process repeats.

Electronic relaxation circuits can be built around a surprising variety of devices. Some of the most popular are:

- ☐ Neon lamps
- ☐ UJTs (UniJunction Transistor)
- ☐ SCRs (Silicon Controlled Rectifiers)
- ☐ Tunnel diodes

It may seem surprising that an electronic signal generator can be built around as humble a component as a simple neon lamp. But the operating characteristics of a neon lamp make it very well suited for relaxation circuits.

A neon lamp is a glass bulb containing a pair of electrodes and a low-pressure inert gas (neon). There are two key threshold voltages that are of concern when working with a neon lamp. When the voltage across the electrodes is low, the gas remains unionized, the resistance between the electrodes is extremely high, and nothing much happens. Increasing the voltage until it passes the main threshold (firing) voltage (Vf) ionizes the gas in the bulb. The gas starts to glow, and the resistance between the two electrodes drops to a very low value. In most cases, some sort of dropping resistor is needed to prevent the lamp from being destroyed by the sudden current surge. Often, a suitable dropping resistor is built right into the lamp's base.

The lamp remains in its activated (glowing) state, even if the voltage across the electrodes drops slightly below Vf. The lamp stays on until the voltage across its electrodes drops below the second threshold (holding) voltage (Vh).

For the NE-83, probably the most popular neon lamp, Vf is typically between 60 to 100 volts, and Vh is about 60 volts. This requirement for a rather high supply voltage tends to limit the practicality of such circuits in modern applications. Still, it is valuable to help you understand just how such circuits function.

A very simple relaxation circuit built around a neon lamp is illustrated in Fig. 1-3. The output frequency is determined both by the R1-C1 time constant, and the difference between the neon lamp's Vf and Vh values.

When power is first applied to the circuit, the neon lamp is unactivated, and exhibits a very high resistance. Capacitor C1 begins to charge. At some point, the voltage across the capacitor (and thus, across the neon lamp) exceeds Vf. The neon lamp is activated. The very low resistance of the neon lamp in its activated state lets the capacitor start to discharge. Before long, the voltage across the capacitor drops below Vh. The neon lamp is cut off, and

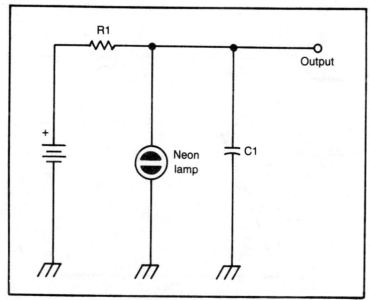

Fig. 1-3. A simple relaxation oscillator can be constructed around a neon lamp.

its resistance goes high again. The capacitor starts to recharge. This cycle repeats endlessly, and the circuit oscillates. The operation of this type of circuit is illustrated in Fig. 1-4.

Many relaxation circuits depend on a curious phenomena known as negative resistance. Ordinary resistance elements obey Ohm's law:

$$E = IR$$

Assuming the resistance is held constant, increasing the voltage applied across the resistance element causes the current flowing through it to increase.

A negative resistance element functions in the opposite manner. Increasing the voltage applied across the negative resistance element causes the current flowing through it to decrease.

A tunnel diode exhibits either positive (normal) resistance or negative resistance under different circumstances. This is illustrated in the characteristic curve graph of Fig. 1-5. Below a specific threshold voltage (Vt), the tunnel diode behaves like an ordinary resistance element. As the voltage increases, the current increases. Above Vf, the tunnel diode exhibits negative resistance. As the voltage increases, the current decreases.

9

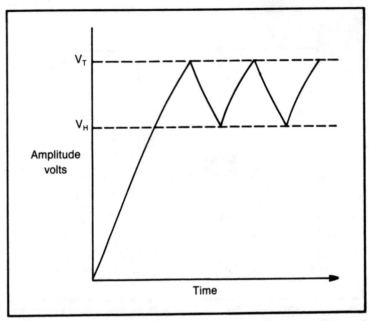

Fig. 1-4. The relaxation oscillator of Fig. 1-3 works by repeatedly charging and discharging a capacitor.

A typical relaxation circuit built around a tunnel diode is shown in Fig. 1-6.

Relaxation oscillators are quite simple and can be useful for certain applications, but feedback oscillators tend to be more flexible and more widely employed in modern circuitry.

However, there is one important modern application for relaxation oscillators—an optoelectronic relaxation oscillator is at the heart of a ruby laser.

FEEDBACK OSCILLATORS

Most practical electronic oscillator circuits are designed around an amplification stage with feedback. The principle is illustrated in block diagram form in Fig. 1-7.

Anyone who has ever worked with a public address amplification system is probably familiar with acoustic feedback. Sound from the speaker is picked up by the microphone, which feeds the signal into the amplifier. The signal's level is amplified and put out through the speaker. The microphone picks up this increased level of sound and feeds it back into the amplifier for more amplification. The output is fed back into the input, creating an

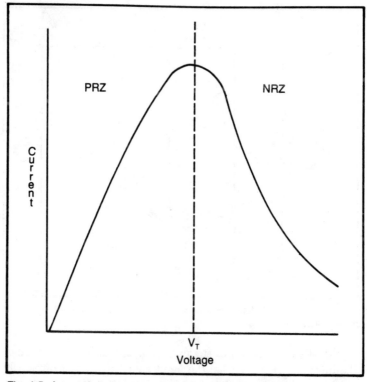

Fig. 1-5. A tunnel diode can exhibit either positive or negative resistance.

endlessly cycling loop. In a PA system this results in a loud, ear-piercing squeal. This is a form of oscillation.

Feedback oscillators take advantage of the same phenomena. A controlled amount of the amplifier's output signal is fed back to the input.

There are actually two basic types of feedback—positive feedback and negative feedback. The differences lies in the phase relationship between the input and output signals. If they are in phase, we have positive feedback. The signal level is continuously amplified to higher and higher amplitudes, subject to the limitations of the amplifier. Positive feedback is the type that can cause the circuit to break into oscillation.

Negative feedback, on the other hand, is out of phase with the original input signal. When out of phase signals are combined, they subtract; that is, their amplitude is decreased rather than increased. Negative feedback is often used in amplifier circuits to control the gain. Negative feedback does not result in oscillations.

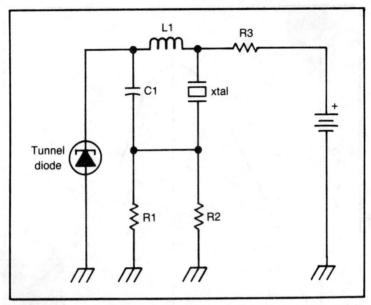

Fig. 1-6. The unique characteristics of a tunnel diode can be put to work in a relaxation oscillator circuit.

Most simple amplifier stages used in oscillator circuits are of the inverting type; that is, the input signal is phase shifted 180 degrees at the amplifier's output. The feedback path must include another 180 degrees of phase shift to obtain positive feedback. There are many ways to do this.

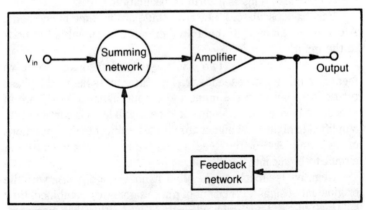

Fig. 1-7. Most practical electronic oscillator circuits consist of an amplification stage with feedback.

The feedback network is also designed to be frequency sensitive. This allows us to determine the exact frequency of the output oscillations. In almost all oscillator circuits, the feedback path includes some sort of resonant network. The concept of resonance is discussed in the following section of this chapter.

Oscillation is always the result of the periodic storage and release of energy. Consider a pendulum, which acts as a mechanical oscillator. Energy is stored as the weight rises, and released as the weight falls. In a feedback oscillator circuit using an inductive-capacitive network, energy is passed back and forth between the inductive and capacitive reactance. Energy is stored in the capacitor, then released through the inductor.

There are a number of basic forms of the feedback oscillator circuit.

☐ Armstrong
☐ Colpitts
☐ crystal
☐ Gunn diode
☐ Hartley
☐ Pierce

These circuit types are discussed in detail in Chapter 2.

RESONANCE

Many electronics hobbyists (and not a few professionals) feel a little intimated when it comes to resonance and impedance. While a bit confusing at first, these vital concepts of electronics theory really aren't so bad once you get used to them.

In a dc circuit, resistance is resistance, and everything is perfectly straightforward. Ohm's law can be used to analyze what is going on throughout the circuit. Ac circuits are a little more complicated, because the polarity of the current flow keeps reversing itself. Moreover, the frequency (number of cycles per second) of the ac signal affects the operating parameters of the circuit.

Ac resistance is called impedance. Impedance is made up of two components: dc resistance, and reactance. The dc resistance is a constant. It is the same, regardless of the applied frequency. Reactance, on the other hand, varies with frequency.

There are two different types of reactance, inductive reactance and capacitive reactance. As the names suggest, an ideal inductor (coil) exhibits only inductive reactance, and an ideal capacitor exhibits only capacitive reactance.

Inductive reactance is determined by the size of the inductance (in henries), and the applied frequency, according to this formula:

$$Xl = 2 \pi FL$$

π, or pi, is a universal constant with an approximate value of 3.14.

Notice that if the frequency increases, the inductive reactance also increases.

Capacitive reactance is determined by the size of the capacitance (in farads) and the applied frequency according to this formula:

$$Xc = 1/2 \pi FC$$

Notice that if the frequency increases, the capacitive reactance decreases. In other words, inductive and capacitive reactance work in opposite directions.

Impedance, or total ac resistance, is the combination of dc resistance, inductive reactance, and capacitive reactance. Because of the phase difference between the two types of reactances, the value cannot be simply added together. The formula for impedance is as follows:

$$Z = \sqrt{R^2 + Xt^2}$$

where Xt is the total reactance.

If the inductive and capacitive reactances are in series, subtract their values:

$$Xt = Xl - Xc$$

Because the total reactance is squared, the sign of the subtraction is essentially irrelevant. The squared value in the impedance equation is always positive. If Xt is negative, the capacitive reactance is larger than the inductive reactance.

If the capacitive and inductive reactances are in parallel, a slightly more complex formula determines the total reactance:

$$Xt = ((Xl)(Xc))/(Xl - Xc)$$

14

At some specific frequency, the capacitive reactance is exactly equal to the inductive reactance. This condition is known as resonance.

For a series circuit, the total reactance is zero. This means the impedance is:

$$Z = \sqrt{R^2 + 0^2}$$
$$Z = \sqrt{R^2}$$
$$Z = R$$

At resonance, the impedance of a series circuit is equal to the dc resistance. If you think about it, this is the lowest value the impedance can have. Below or above resonance, the impedance is greater than the dc resistance.

In a parallel circuit, at resonance the total reactance is essentially infinity. The impedance is also nearly infinite. Obviously, this is the maximum possible value of the impedance in the circuit.

In a series-resonant circuit, the impedance is at a minimum at resonance. In a parallel-resonant circuit, the impedance is at a maximum at resonance.

The resonant frequency is the same for both series and parallel circuits. The resonant frequency can be found with this formula:

$$F = 1/(2 \pi \sqrt{LC})$$

This formula can be rearranged to find suitable component values. If you know the desired resonant frequency, and the inductance you can find the necessary capacitance with this formula:

$$C = 1/(4 \pi^2 f^2 L)$$

$4 \pi^2$ is approximately 39.5, so the formula can be re-written as:

$$C = 1/(39.5F^2 L)$$

Similarly, if you chose the capacitance first, the required inductance can be found with this formula:

$$L = 1/(4 \pi^2 F^2 C)$$

or with this one:

$$L = 1/(39.5F^2 C)$$

15

Resonant circuits aren't always built around separate capacitors and coils. For examples, a crystal is a one-piece resonant network. Both series-resonant and parallel-resonant crystals are available.

In an oscillator circuit, the resonant network is most willing to oscillate at its characteristic resonant frequency.

APPLICATIONS

Many different types of oscillator and signal generator circuits have been developed. The oscillator/signal generator is one of the most frequently used electronic sub-circuits.

It is impossible to list all of the possible applications for oscillators and signal generators. I will quickly mention just a few typical applications:

☐ Testing (discussed in the next section of this chapter)
☐ Horizontal and vertical oscillators in a TV set
☐ Carrier generation for radio transmission
☐ Carrier recreation for radio reception.
☐ Creating sounds (for alarms, electronic music, code practice oscillators, etc.)
☐ Clocks and timers
☐ Electronic pattern generation
☐ Sensing (radar, ultrasonic intrusion detection, etc.)
☐ Insect repellers
☐ Lasers

TEST EQUIPMENT

Oscillators and signal generators are useful for many types of electronic testing including:

☐ Signal injection/tracing to locate defects
☐ Impedance measurement
☐ Distortion measurement
☐ Gain measurement
☐ Frequency response measurement

Several standard pieces of test equipment are basically just high-quality, controllable signal generators. A well-stocked electronics workbench contains one or more of the following:

☐ Audio oscillator

☐ Rf signal generator
☐ Function generator
☐ Pulse generator

The Audio Oscillator

The audio oscillator is a popular piece of test equipment. Used to check audio equipment, such as amplifiers and tape recorders. The audio oscillator generates clean, precise signals in the audible range (approximately 20 Hz to 20 kHz). Figure 1-8 shows a block diagram of a basic audio oscillator.

Most audio oscillators generate sine waves. Some offer additional waveforms, such as square waves. When several waveforms can be selected, the audio oscillator is more properly called a function generator (discussed shortly).

These low-distortion, low-noise signals are primarily used to design and service high quality audio equipment. The prime requirement for much serious audio work is a high purity signal. A good audio oscillator generates a signal of extremely low harmonic content and low noise.

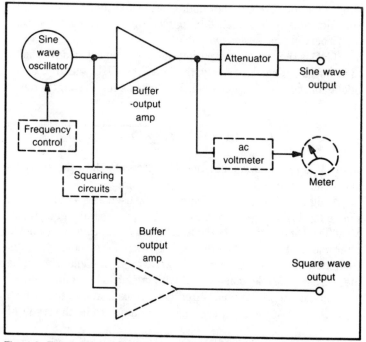

Fig. 1-8. The audio oscillator is a very useful piece of test equipment.

Most high quality audio oscillators have a metering circuit connected at the power amplifier output which allows the operator to precisely adjust the output level settings with the variable attenuator. Some higher-priced audio oscillators permit synchronization of the audio oscillator frequency to an external standard. This is useful when a high degree of frequency or phase relationship control is necessary.

Most audio oscillators do not offer a true square wave output, but many do provide a limited square wave output for triggering oscilloscopes or synchronizing other equipment. In practice, the difference between a synchronizing output and a true square wave output may be subtle. A synchronizing output is more limited and offers less control than a true square wave output. A synchronizing output does have an output attenuator, a constant or controlled output impedance, controlled output amplitude or a symmetric (duty cycle) control.

Until fairly recently, an audio oscillator that could generate a sinusoidal signal with a 0.25 percent THD (Total Harmonic Distortion) was perfectly adequate for audio equipment design and service. But audio equipment has become increasingly sophisticated. Today the audio oscillator must have THD specifications of less than 0.05 percent and preferably less than 0.025 percent for serious work.

THD is the amount of spurious harmonic energy a device adds to its output signal. Obviously, the lower the THD, the greater the fidelity of the device in question. The formula for THD (in percent) is:

$$\%THD = (H \times 100)/ \sqrt{(F \times F) + (H \times H)}$$

where F is the fundamental, and H represents all of the spurious harmonic content.

A high quality audio oscillator can be used as a known signal source for THD measurements of amplifiers, or similar equipment. Most THD analyzers reject the fundamental frequency with a notch filter and measure all the other energy within the audio spectrum contained in the output signal. Clearly, the test signal should be the purest possible sine wave, with an absolute minimum of harmonic content. Any measured harmonics in the output which were not part of the input signal are presumed to be the result of THD.

Great care must be taken in performing such tests. If the

generator drifts from the fundamental frequency to which the analyzer was tuned, errors can occur in the analysis.

Any hum in the output signal can also cause problems with the THD measurement. Hum is misinterpreted by the analyzer as spurious harmonic distortion. Therefore, all ground loops must be carefully avoided. A ground loop is a second path through which the ground or return signals for the test may pass. Frequently, this second ground path also contains significant line-frequency currents, which enter into the measurement and contribute undesired components to the output signal. A ground loop hum is generated by neither the amplifier under test, nor the signal source (oscillator), but it still affects the measurement, resulting in false THD readings.

Another type of distortion that can show up in an amplifier is InterModulation Distortion (IMD). Like THD, IMD occurs when there are non-linearities in the circuitry. The spurious signals in this case are not harmonics of the fundamental. They are the sum and difference products of two or more amplified signals.

An audio oscillator can also be used to drive an audio amplifier to a desired output level to make power measurements, or to measure the audio frequency response of an amplifier or other audio equipment.

Both input and output measurements can be made by using an audio oscillator as a signal source. These measurements are usually made by first establishing an output voltage level from the amplifier, and either insert a variable series resistance for input impedance measurements, or a variable parallel load resistance for output impedance measurements. The inserted resistance is then adjusted until the output voltage is reduced by 50 percent (6 dB). At this point, the resistance setting is equal to the unknown impedance.

In working with audio amplifiers, damping factors must also be considered. The damping factor of an audio amplifier is the ratio of the output impedance to the rated load impedance. An amplifier whose output impedance is perfectly matched to the load impedance has a damping factor of 1. Practical audio amplifiers generally have damping factors of about 50, or greater.

The damping factor of an amplifier can be measured by driving the unloaded amplifier to its maximum output without introducing distortion. The no-load output value is called Vnl. Next, the rated load (usually 4, 8, or 16 ohms) is connected to the amplifier, and the full load output voltage is now measured (Vfl). The damping factor can now be calculated from the results of these two measurements, using this formula:

$$\text{Damping factor} = Vfl/(Vnl - Vfl)$$

Many better-quality audio oscillators offer synchronization capabilities. In the synchronization mode, the audio oscillator can be used for signal regeneration. In many laboratory situations, processing or measurement can cause the measured signal regeneration. In many laboratory situations, processing or measurement can cause the measured signal to become too noisy, too high in distortion, or to have excessive amplitude variations. Applying the potentially troublesome signal to the synchronizing input of an audio oscillator results in an output signal in which noise, distortion, and amplitude variations are highly suppressed. If desired, a limited amount of phase shift can be added by adjusting the front panel variable frequency control.

It is important to remember that the synchronizing input of an audio oscillator does not reject harmonics. The audio oscillator can easily be locked onto the second, third, fourth, fifth, or even higher harmonics of the synchronizing signal, if the harmonic amplitude is high enough. In some applications this may be desirable. In other applications, it may be a problem to be avoided.

Other measurements that can be made with an audio oscillator include:

☐ Input sensitivity
☐ Input overload
☐ Bridge measurements

(The audio oscillator must have a balanced output to make bridge measurements.)

It should be very clear that the audio oscillator is an extremely versatile piece of test equipment.

Rf Signal Generator

The rf signal generator is similar in principle to the audio oscillator. The main difference is in the frequency range covered. An audio oscillator generates frequencies in the audible region (below about 20 kHz). A rf signal generator produces frequencies in the rf (Radio Frequency) region, typically 50 kHz to 10 MHz. By definition, the lower limit is above 20 kHz (the upper limit of the audio region. The upper frequency limit can be as high as 1

GHz. If signals above 1 GHz are needed, a special class of rf generator called a microwave signal source is used.

Despite the name, rf signal generators are true oscillators, producing sine wave signals via feedback circuits. Certain basic features are found on most rf signal generators including:

- ☐ Adjustable frequency range
- ☐ Modulation capability (AM, FM, and/or pulse)
- ☐ Amplitude control
- ☐ Wide range of output amplitude control

Most rf signal generators offer the ability to generate signals as low as 1 μV or less.

Rf signal generators usually fall into one or two general price categories. Less expensive units typically sell for below $200. Better quality rf signal generators usually run somewhere between $1000 and $10,000. For some reason, very few rf signal generators are available in the $200 to $1000 range.

As with audio oscillators, rf signal generators have become increasingly sophisticated and offer better specifications to match the increased sophistication of the products the generators are used with. Somewhat surprisingly, there has been relatively little change in the price range of rf generators over the years. This is one of the few cases where you can get more for the same price.

In recent years, the communications industry has changed vhf and uhf standards from wideband FM deviation (± 5 kHz) to narrowband deviation (± 3 kHz). Today's technicians need generators with precise modulation capability and substantially improved frequency stability requirements.

As a rule, low-cost generators fill most of the needs of the home experimenter and adequately supply the rf signals required by the service shop for simple alignment procedures.

The simplest rf signal generators are power oscillators that use a fixed inductor and a variable capacitor as the frequency determining elements. Low cost units usually lack the stability, rf shielding, frequency range, and modulation capability required to verify performance specifications when servicing or calibrating communications, industrial, or high-fidelity equipment. For this type of work, a more deluxe rf signal generator is required.

The highest quality rf signal generators employ sophisticated synthesis circuits that deliver signals of high spectral purity, extreme stability, and uniform modulation capability.

Somewhat less expensive rf signal generators are built around the LC (inductance-capacitance) oscillator with stages of buffering, modulation and power amplification. This basic approach is found at the upper end of the lower price range and the lower end of the higher priced group. LC type rf signal generators that cover 50 MHz to 100 MHz usually employ the Hartley oscillator.

The frequency generated by a LC oscillator is directly related to the square root of the capacitance and inductance. In the Hartley oscillator the inductor is fixed, and the capacitor is variable. When the desired frequency can no longer be reached by adjusting the capacitor, a new inductor is switch-selected. A large capacitive change is required to obtain a reasonable frequency range before a band change is required. Band ranges on most rf signal generators using LC oscillators typically cover a frequency spread of about 3:1.

Some rf signal generators employ the Colpitts oscillator which is based on a split capacitance, rather than a split inductance. Unfortunately, this type of oscillator does not provide as wide a tuning range as the Hartley oscillator.

Not surprisingly, the stability and spectral purity of the output of a rf signal generator output is largely dependent on the characteristics of the LC circuit. A high Q (quality factor) circuit designed with silver plated coils and air variable capacitors is often used.

Extensive decoupling circuitry is commonly used on all power supply connections. This serves two purposes. First, the decoupling circuitry keeps external signals from modulating the oscillator and therefore creating undesirable spurious signals. Secondly, it removes the desired signal from the power supply lines, so the signal is not radiated except through connections to the output attenuator terminals.

When uhf signals are needed, the LC oscillator becomes hard to use. Stray inductance and capacitance must be reduced to a absolute minimum to reach the highest frequencies. A practical alternative to the LC oscillator for uhf applications is to employ either the cavity or shortened transmission line. In either type, the fundamental signal is no longer developed by independent inductance and capacitance, but uses the lump constant characteristics of transmission lines or coaxial cavities instead.

The cavity has considerably higher Q than a LC circuit. The major disadvantage of the cavity is the awkward size. Cavity dimensions may run from one quarter of a wavelength to a full wavelength, thus making the cavity unsuitable for operation below

300 to 400 MHz. Also, cavities can't be easily bandswitched, so other techniques must be used in generators that must cover a wide range of frequencies. One such technique is illustrated in Fig. 1-9. The output of the cavity and the output of a fixed frequency oscillator are mixed to generate a lower frequency signal. Both the cavity and the fixed frequency oscillator operate at a considerably higher frequency than the desired generator output. Even though only one oscillator is shown as a variable frequency cavity, both oscillators may be variable frequency cavities in certain generator designs. Modern cavity circuits are usually electronically tuned by an extremely high quality variable-capacitance diode. These techniques require only simple feedback circuits to maintain frequency stability.

When an LC oscillator is used as the heart of a rf signal generator, it is housed in a sturdy casing that shields it, and provides a stable mechanical and temperature environment. Figure 1-10 is a block diagram of a basic rf signal generator using a band-switched LC oscillator. The oscillator drives a buffer amplifier that helps maintain frequency stability with changes in the output load. The buffer amplifier may be omitted on some low-cost units.

A power amplifier is used to drive the 50-ohm impedance lines, even though the signal from the basic oscillator/buffer may be at a sufficient amplitude required of the generator output. The amplifier supplies the maximum possible signal to the output attenuator. The maximum level is usually in the 1 to 3 volt range. The attenuator then reduces the output signal to a level selected by the operator.

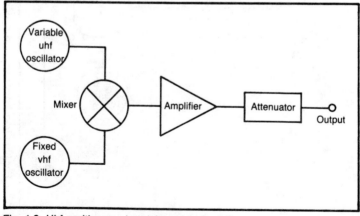

Fig. 1-9. Uhf cavities can be tricky to bandswitch.

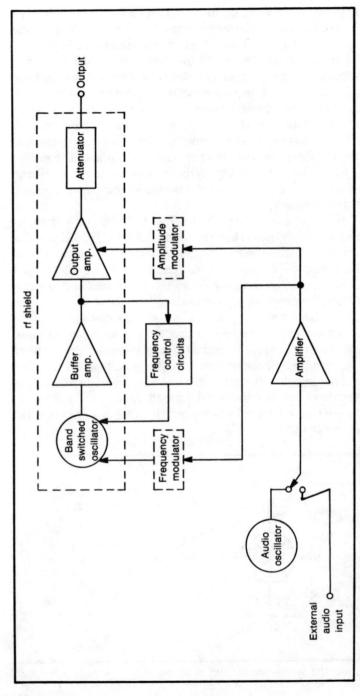

Fig. 1-10. For high frequency testing, a rf signal generator is used.

24

There is extensive shielding around these four sections to prevent stray signals from leaking from any one of these circuit sections. The shielding is usually a rather complex mechanical design. A box within a box is often employed.

Some of the sections included in the block diagram do not appear in all designs. These optional sections are shown as dashed boxes.

Most rf signal generators contain some form of modulator. AM (Amplitude Modulation) and FM (Frequency Modulation) are the most common forms of modulation. Rf signal generators with upper frequency limits in the 30 MHz to 60 MHz region generally offer AM only. Most signal generators with FM capability also have AM capability. Some generators, especially those designed for work in the high vhf and uhf region, also have pulse modulation capability. Pulse modulation is 0 to 100 percent AM in the form of a square wave or pulse.

AM (Amplitude Modulation) is applied to either the output amplifier, or some modulator ahead of the output amplifier. A few generators modulate ahead of the output amplifier. A few generators modulate the oscillator directly. The modulator receives audio signals from an internal oscillator or an external source. On higher quality generators, the audio oscillator provides tones of 400 Hz and 1 kHz. Simpler generators offer only one tone.

In generators featuring FM (frequency modulation), signals from the modulating oscillator are applied to the frequency modulating components of the bandswitch oscillator. This is usually done through circuitry that maintains a constant deviation, regardless of the oscillator frequency setting.

In a few of the deluxe, most expensive rf signal generators, frequency-control circuitry monitors the output frequency, compares it to a standard, and applies corrective signals to the bandswitch oscillator. This action maintains the desired frequency setting.

Function Generators

Conceptually, the function generator is similar to the audio oscillator, and it is used for many of the same applications. The major difference is that the function generator offers a choice of output waveforms, usually triangle waves and rectangle waves are available. Some function generators also put out sine waves and/or sawtooth waves. Occasionally, additional waveforms are also provided.

The function generator first appeared in laboratory use in the 1950s. The first function generators were very expensive instruments, often costing several thousand dollars. By the 1970s, a function generator of similar capabilities could be purchased for under $300. Today, prices for basic function generators have dropped to the $100 range.

Function generators usually cover a wide frequency range. A 0.1 Hz to 1 MHz range is not at all unusual.

A block diagram of a typical function generator is shown in Fig. 1-11. The signal starts out as a triangle wave. All other waveforms are derived from the basic triangle wave signal.

The triangle wave generator is the heart of function generator. Its design is usually based on the special voltage-time characteristics of a capacitor charged by a constant-current source. If there is no stray resistance across the capacitor (this requirement is usually met by using extremely low-leakage capacitors) the voltage across the capacitor increases linearly as time increases. This curve is reversed when capacitor is discharged. This allows a triangle wave generator to be created by first charging a capacitor with a constant-current source until a desired positive peak voltage is reached. Then the charging constant-current source is turned off and a discharging (opposite polarity) constant-current source is turned on. When the voltage across the capacitor is reduced to the desired negative peak, the circuit switches back to its original state and the cycle repeats. The triangle wave signal is passed through a sine shaper circuit to create a sine wave with only 0.5% to 2% THD.

A squaring circuit is used to derive a square wave from the original triangle wave signal. This derived square wave is 90

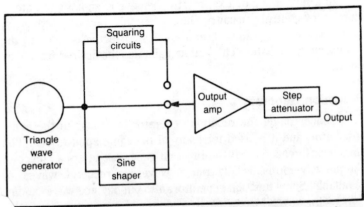

1-11. A function generator can put out any of several different waveforms.

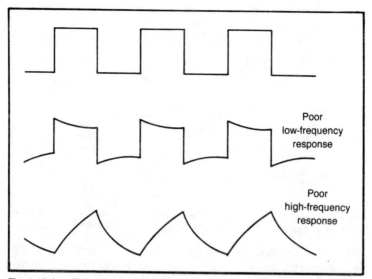

Fig. 1-12. Insufficient frequency response can significantly distort a square wave signal.

degrees out of phase with the triangle wave zero crossing. This phase relationship is constant.

The function generator's multiple waveshapes permit more convenient testing of distortion and frequency response. Distortion of a waveform is more obvious when the wave is made up of straight lines and sharp angles. The smooth curves of a sine wave can mask some minor distortion.

In addition, the multiple frequency components of complex waveforms can also simplify frequency response measurement. Any low-frequency or high-frequency roll-off is apparent as distortion of the waveshape. Figure 1-12 shows some typical distortion effects on a square wave.

An amp driven by triangle wave reveals a great deal about its characteristics if the input and output waveforms are compared. When viewing the signals on an oscilloscope, even simple gain measurements can be made more precisely with a triangle wave. A sine wave is inherently more ambiguous. A triangle has a very precise peak. Crossover distortion also becomes very apparent with a triangle wave. This affect is illustrated in Fig. 1-13.

The proper technique for analyzing problems in servo systems is to break the loop at some convenient point and substitute a theoretically correct signal at that point. A function generator is an ideal source of substitute signals at almost any frequency. The

27

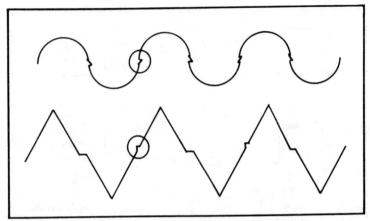

Fig. 1-13. Crossover distortion is very easy to spot in a triangle wave.

output of a function generator is generally at a sufficiently low impedance to simulate virtually any source without introducing special characteristics of its own. Function generators with an adjustable dc offset is even more suited for this type of job. Many servo systems have dc offsets.

The function generator is usually used with an oscilloscope to monitor the returning signal at the break point. A dual-trace scope is preferred. Such an instrument permits simultaneous examination of the input and output signals.

Pulse Generators

The pulse generator is quite similar to the function generator. As the name suggests, the pulse generator's chief function is to produce high quality pulse, or rectangle, waveforms.

As discussed earlier in this chapter, a pulse consists of a fundamental frequency plus a great number of even and odd harmonic components. The harmonic components have specific phase relationships with each other, as well as with the fundamental frequency. If that phase relationship is not precisely maintained, the waveform of the pulse deteriorates. If an essentially stable pulse waveform is passed through an amplifier, the amplifier's output can then be examined for any aberrations. Any such aberrations indicate that the phase response of the amplifier is not uniform. For example, if there are any peaks and/or valleys in the amplifier's frequency-response curve, usually caused by either leading or lagging reactive elements in the circuit, the problem shows up in the output pulse wave. If the pulse wave is distorted at the amplifier's output, further analysis with a sweep generator or a low distortion audio oscilloscope is needed.

Using a pulse generator as the signal source can simplify many of the measurements that are often made when testing analog circuits. Generally speaking, pulse generators are useful over a wide frequency range. This can certainly come in very handy when working with broadband amplifiers and similar equipment. For instance, a single conventional pulse generator is the only signal source needed to fully test an amplifier whose frequency response extends from below 1 Hz to considerably more than 10 kHz. The only alternative might be testing that amplifier with an audio oscillator for the low end and an rf generator for the upper end—or perhaps a very wide-range function generator. The pulse generator can handle the job more simply and more quickly.

The pulse's fast rise and fall times are caused by the pulse's high-frequency components, while the interval between the rise and fall times (i.e., the top of the pulse) is caused by the low-frequency components. In some cases, the frequency of those components is so low that it approaches dc. Those high and low frequency components are what gives the pulse generator its wide frequency range. In addition, the type of waveshape distortion indicates the approximate problem area in the frequency response.

Generally, frequency response measurements for an amplifier are made at the 3 dB points, or the point at which the amplifier delivers half its rated power output, or 70 percent of its rated voltage output. That 3 dB-point is considered the upper and lower cutoff frequency of the amplifier.

The simplest method for measuring the low-frequency 3 dB cutoff is by adjusting the pulse generator so that the pulse droop (the difference between the amplitude immediately following the leading edge and the amplitude at which the trailing edge begins) is 25 percent. Pulse droop is expressed as a percentage of the amplitude at the leading edge, illustrated in Fig. 1-14.

When the pulse droop is adjusted at 25 percent, the width of the pulse is related to the frequency of the lower 3 dB point according to this formula (t is the width of the pulse):

$$F_{low} = 0.0456/t$$

The constant (0.456) is derived from a Fourier analysis of the pulse.

The formula for the upper 3 dB cutoff is:

$$F_{high} = 0.35/Tr$$

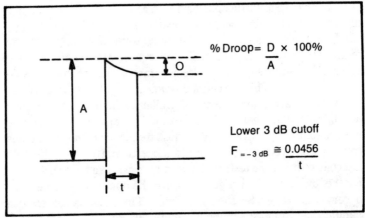

% Droop= $\dfrac{D}{A}$ × 100%

Lower 3 dB cutoff

$F_{=-3\,dB} \cong \dfrac{0.0456}{t}$

Fig. 1-14. Pulse droop is a good indicator of the low-frequency 3 dB point.

Tr is the pulse rise time. All times are in nanoseconds: frequencies are in Hz.

Both of these formulas are just approximations, and do not give exact values. Fortunately precise values are rarely needed for this type of work.

Rise time measurements can be used to approximately measure the upper-frequency response limits of a broadband amplifier. A few precautions must be taken when making this type of measurement. Consider the effect of the test setup itself. Each part of the setup plays a role in determining the rise time of the output that is displayed on the oscilloscope. The rise time of the pulse is changed slightly as it passes through the various components in the test setup. The displayed rise time, therefore, is actually a function of the rise times through each part of that setup:

$$Tr = 1.1 \times \text{square root of } (Tg + Ta + Tp + To)$$

Tr is the display rise time
Tg is the rise time of the pulse generator squared
Ta is the rise time of the amplifier under test squared
Tp is the rise time of the probe squared
To is the rise time of the oscilloscope squared

Because of its extremely fast rise time, a pulse generator can be used to make propagation delay and phase delay measurements relatively convenient and easy. Any circuit (either analog or digital) inevitably introduces some fixed time delay to signals that pass through it. No circuit can pass a signal instantaneously. The delay is called the propagation delay.

Generally, the most practical way to measure propagation delay is to use a dual-trace oscilloscope and a pulse generator. The phase difference between the input and output signals reveals the propagation delay.

Like the function generator, the pulse generator can be made more powerful and versatile by adding special features. Many pulse generators include a delay generator and have a special mode in which an additional pulse is output. That additional pulse is derived from either the trigger circuitry or the basic pulse-rate generator. The purpose of this secondary output is to signal external devices that a pulse is about to be generated, permitting synchronization. In many units, the synchronization pulse preceeds the generation of the main pulse by 20 to 40 nanoseconds, allowing an oscilloscope or other device to start operating on the incoming pulse. Some pulse generators use a square wave for the synchronization signal, while others employ a narrow pulse. In either case, a specific edge is used as the trigger edge; the other edge of the waveform has no particular significance.

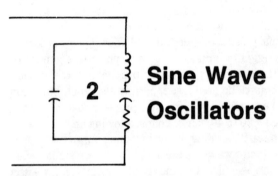

Sine Wave Oscillators

2

THE MOST BASIC WAVEFORM IS THE SINE WAVE. THERE IS JUST one frequency component (the fundamental). There are no harmonics.

While it's easy to visualize, generating a pure sine wave is not always an easy task. Most practical sine wave oscillators produce a few harmonics, along with the fundamental. However, it isn't too difficult to generate a sine wave that is good enough for most practical applications. This chapter looks at some of the most common ways to generate a sine wave.

LC PARALLEL RESONANT TANKS

Most sine wave oscillator circuits are built around parallel resonant LC circuits. This is nothing more than an inductor (coil) and a capacitor connected in parallel. The fundamental operations of a LC oscillator are illustrated in Fig. 2-1.

When the switch is closed, as in Fig. 2-1A, the voltage through coil L1 rapidly increases from zero to the source voltage. Of course, this means that the current through the coil also must be increasing. According to the principle of induction, a change of current through a coil generate a magnetic field. This magnetic field induces a similar voltage in L2, which is stored by capacitor C.

When the current through L1 reaches a stable point and stops increasing, the magnetic field generator around this coil collapses. This means no further voltage is induced into L2, and C can

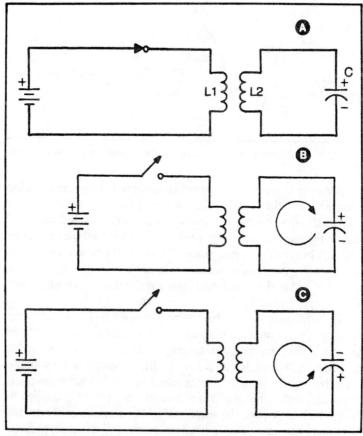

Fig. 2-1. Most sine wave oscillator circuits are built around a parallel resonant LC tank

discharge through the coil in the opposite direction from the original voltage.

This discharge voltage now causes L2 to induce a voltage into L1, which in turn induces the voltage back into L2, charging C in the opposite direction, illustrated in Fig. 2-1B. Once the induced voltage in the coils collapses, this whole discharge/charge process repeats with the polarities again reversed, as shown in Fig. 2-1C.

Theoretically, this cycling back and forth between the capacitance and the inductances will continue indefinitely. In real world components, the coils and the capacitor have some dc resistance which decreases the amplitude on each new oscillation cycle. The signal is eventually damped out, as illustrated in Fig. 2-2.

In addition to dc resistance, any energy that is tapped out of

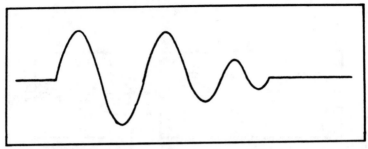

Fig. 2-2. Without some form of amplification, the oscillations are soon damped out.

the circuit to be used by another circuit subtracts from the available energy within the LC circuit. Due to these losses, a point is soon reached when the signal level is too weak to feed back and sustain the oscillations. For this reason, practical feedback oscillator circuits always incorporate some kind of amplification stage. The output of the oscillator is continuously fed back to the input of the amplifier, and so the signal amplitude is maintained at a usable level. This is called positive (in phase) feedback.

It might seem at first that the amplifier would keep increasing the output amplitude indefinitely; but all practical amplifiers have natural limitations that prevent any further increases beyond a specific output level, which is linked with the supply voltage of the amplifier circuit. In an oscillator, the amplifier's saturation point is reached within a few cycles of the time the power is applied to the circuit. After that, the amplitude of the output signal remains essentially constant. This is a natural characteristic of amplifiers.

Another natural characteristic of amplifiers is often taken advantage of to start the oscillations in the first place. All amplifiers generate some internal noise, and produce a tiny output signal even if the input is perfectly grounded. This noise can be fed back through the amplifier until its amplitude is increased to a level that can start oscillations within the LC tank.

The frequency of the oscillations is determined by the resonant frequency of the specific coil-capacitor combination used. The formula is:

$$F = 1/(6.28 \sqrt{LC})$$

F is the frequency in hertz, L is the inductance in henries, and C is the capacitance in farads. The constant 6.28 is an approximation for two times pi (2π).

34

As explained in Chapter 1, at resonance the reactance of the capacitor is equal to the reactance of the inductor. As frequency is increased, inductive reactance increases, while capacitive reactance decreases. Only at resonance (equal reactances) can oscillations be sustained.

This basic formula is applicable for any oscillator circuit built around a LC parallel resonant tank. Because this formula is important, let's work through a typical example to give you a feel for how it works.

Let's assume we have a LC parallel resonant circuit made up of a 30 μF (0.00003 farad) capacitor and a 150 mH (0.15 henry) coil. The resonant frequency is about equal to:

$$
\begin{aligned}
F &= 1/(6.28 \sqrt{(0.15 \times 0.00003)} \\
&= 1/(6.28 \sqrt{0.0000045)} \\
&= 1/(6.28 \times 0.0021213) \\
&= 1/0.0133217 \\
&= 75 \text{ Hz.}
\end{aligned}
$$

For a second example, let's use the same inductance (0.15 henry), but change the capacitance to 0.75 μF (0.00000075 farad). This time the resonant frequency works out to approximately;

$$
\begin{aligned}
F &= 1/(6.28 \sqrt{(0.15 \times 0.00000075}} \\
&= 1/(6.28 \sqrt{0.0000112} \\
&= 1/(6.28 \times 0.0003346 \\
&= 1/0.0021012 \\
&= 476 \text{ Hz.}
\end{aligned}
$$

Decreasing the value of either component (the capacitance, or the inductance) increases the resonant frequency.

THE HARTLEY OSCILLATOR

One of the most common types of LC parallel resonant feedback oscillator circuit is the Hartley oscillator. A typical circuit is shown in Fig. 2-3. This circuit is often referred to as a split-inductance oscillator because coil L is center-tapped. In effect, L acts like two separate coils in very close proximity. A current through coil section AB induces a signal into coil section BC.

When power is first applied to this circuit, resistor R2 places a small negative voltage on the base of the transistor, allowing it to conduct. Internal noise builds up within the transistor

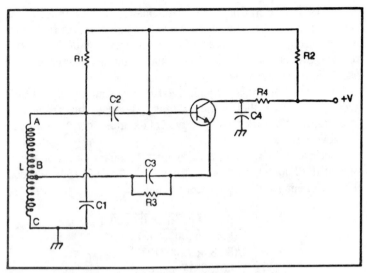

Fig. 2-3. The Hartley oscillator uses a split inductance.

amplification stage, as described above. When this noise signal reaches a usable level, current from the transistor's collector passes through resistors R4, R2, and R1. This rising current finally reaches coil section AB, inducing a voltage into coil section BC. The induced voltage is stored by capacitor C1.

Capacitor C2 is selected to have a very low impedance at the oscillating frequency. In effect, the base of the transistor is connected more or less directly to C1. The base voltage provided by R2 is quite low, so it can be reasonably ignored once oscillations have been started. This connection is needed only to initiate the oscillation process.

As capacitor C1 charges, it increases the bias on the transistor. This in turn increases the current through coil section AB, and the induced voltage through coil section BC. At the same time, the charge on both C1 and C2 is also increased.

Eventually, the voltage across C1 equals the R1/C2 voltage, but with the opposite polarity. In other words, these voltages now completely cancel each other out. At this point, the transistor is saturated. Its output now stops rising, so the magnetic field around coil section AB collapses. No further voltage is induced into coil section BC.

Capacitor C1 now starts to discharge through coil section BC, allowing C2 to discharge through R1, cutting off the transistor until the next cycle begins.

Naturally, it takes some time for C1 to discharge through coil section BC. Therefore, as the current through the coil is increased, it builds up a magnetic field. Once the capacitor is discharged it stops supplying current to the coil, but the coil tends to oppose the change in current flow. It continues to conduct, charging the capacitor in the opposite direction, and the entire process is repeated.

In some applications, the low impedance of the transistor may load the tank circuit excessively, increasing power loss, and possibly decreasing the stability of the circuit. This problem can be overcome by substituting a high impedance active device, such as a FET, as illustrated in Fig. 2-4. Except for the increased impedance, the operation of this circuit is the same as the standard version built around a bipolar transistor.

The transistor in a Hartley oscillator is connected in the common-collector configuration. That is, the transistor's collector is at ac ground potential because of the presence of the bypass capacitor.

A practical Hartley oscillator circuit is shown in Fig. 2-5.

THE COLPITTS OSCILLATOR

A close relative of the Hartley oscillator is the Colpitts oscillator, illustrated in Fig. 2-6. Where the Hartley oscillator is based on a split-inductance, the Colpitts oscillator employs a split-capacitance.

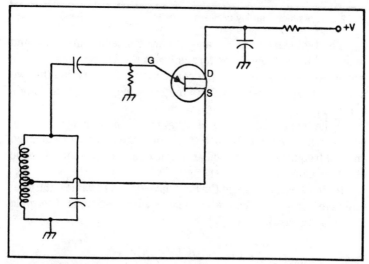

Fig. 2-4. A high impedance device, such as a FET, can help minimize loading problems.

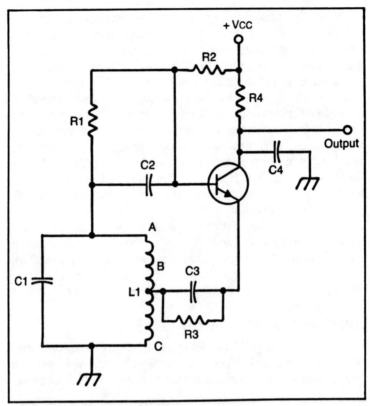

Fig. 2-5. A practical Hartley oscillator circuit.

The two capacitors (C1 and C2) are connected in series, and function like a single capacitor, as far as the LC resonant tank is concerned. The center tap (the connection point between the two individual capacitors) provides a feedback loop to the transistor's emitter.

If the two capacitors are of equal value, the total effective capacitance within the LC tank (determining the resonant frequency, and the frequency of the oscillations) is equal to one half the value of either capacitor separately.

If the two capacitors in the tank have different values, the total effective capacitance can be calculated with the standard formula for capacitances in series;

$$1/C_t = 1/C_1 + 1/C_2$$

In practical Colpitts circuits, the two capacitors are usually not equal, because the strength of the feedback signal is dependent on the ratio of these two capacitances. By changing both of these capacitor values in inverse fashion (increasing one, while decreasing the other by a like amount) the feedback level can be varied, while the resonant frequency is held constant.

This brings up one of the chief limitations of the Colpitts oscillator. It is not always convenient to change the oscillation frequency in operation. When the frequency is changed, you obviously don't want the feedback signal to vary, or the amplitude of the output signal will not be constant, and oscillations may not be sustained in the circuit. This is not an insurmountable problem, just an inconvenience. Both capacitances must be changed simultaneously, requiring a hard-to-find ganged variable capacitor.

It might seem that you could just make the coil adjustable instead of the capacitors. After all, changing either the inductance or the capacitance in the tank permits control of the resonant frequency. This is true enough on the theoretical level, but in most applications is just as impractical. Without getting into unnecessary detail, a general rule of thumb is that it is generally preferable to use an adjustable capacitor rather than an adjustable inductor.

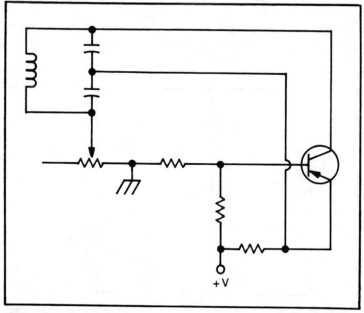

Fig. 2-6. The Colpitts oscillator is similar to the Hartley oscillator, except that it uses a split capacitance.

A frequent solution in practical Colpitts circuits is to add a third variable capacitance in parallel with the fixed series capacitances, shown in Fig. 2-7. This technique keeps the C1:C2 ratio constant, since both of these capacitors have fixed values, but the resonant frequency is variable. The total effective capacitance in the tank is dependant on all three capacitors—C1, C2, and C3. The formula for the total effective tank capacitance is;

$$Ct = C3 + 1/\left[(1/C1)+(1/C2)\right]$$

The Colpitts oscillator is a very popular circuit, because it offers very good frequency stability at a reasonable cost. Like the Hartley oscillator, the Colpitts oscillator places the transistor in the common-collector configuration.

Here's the step-by-step design procedure for a typical Colpitts oscillator. The first step is to decide on the circuit's specifications. In this case, we will aim for the following specifications;

$$V_{CC} = 9 \text{ volts}$$
$$\text{output frequency} = 10 \text{ kHz. (10,000 Hz.)}$$
$$\text{output power} = 35 \text{ mW (0.035 watt)}$$

The amplifier stage will be operated in class A for maximum stability. (This is common for oscillator circuits.)

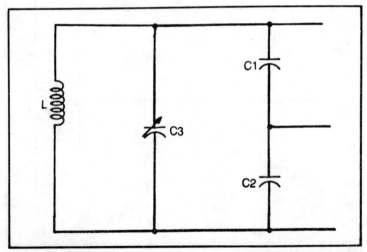

Fig. 2-7. A third variable capacitor in parallel with the fixed series capacitances permits manual tuning of the output frequency.

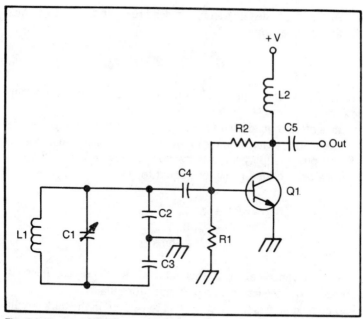

Fig. 2-8. A practical Colpitts oscillator circuit.

You can design our oscillator around the standardized circuit diagram shown in Fig. 2-8. Use a HEP-50 general purpose NPN transistor for the circuit, primarily because this device is readily available. A partial specification sheet for this transistor is given in Table 2-1.

Table 2-1. A Partial Specification Sheet for a HEP-50 Transistor.

TYPE	NPN
β	85
ABSOLUTE MAXIMUM RATINGS	
POWER	400 mW (0.4 watt)
I_c (Collector current)	
	300 mA (0.3 ampere)
V_{cb}	25 volts
V_{ce}	15 volts
V_{eb}	4.0 volts
FREQUENCY RESPONSE 250 MHz (250,000,000 Hz)	

According to design theory, the load resistance of the LC tank should be equal to;

$$R1 = V_{CC} / 2P_o$$

where V_{CC} is the supply voltage, and P_o is the desired output power.

It is often a good idea to cut back on the V_{CC} voltage a little in this equation to leave some margin for error. Since you are using a 9 volt power supply (or battery) you can lower V_{CC} to 8 volts. This makes the load resistance equal to;

$$\begin{aligned} R1 &= 8 / (2 \times 0.035) \\ &= 64/0.07 \\ &= 914 \text{ ohms} \end{aligned}$$

For convenience, round this value off to 900 ohms. There is no need for precision in this particular formula.

The next step is to select the coil to be used in the tank circuit (L1). For this application, you need to give some consideration to the Q (Quality factor) of the coil. Q is the ratio between the dc resistance and the ac reactance. For a series resistance, the formula is;

$$Q = X/R_s$$

For a parallel resistance, it is:

$$Q = R_p/X$$

The Q has a definite effect on the bandwidth of the circuit. F is the output frequency (resonant frequency of the tank), and BW is the bandwidth.

$$BW = F/Q$$

For most oscillator circuits, you will usually want a Q of about 10 to 20. In the sample design, let's use a Q of 20.

To find the Q imposed on the coil by paralleling it with a 900 ohm load (R1), use the parallel form of the Q equation, and rearrange it to solve for the desired reactance;

$$Q = R_p/X$$

$$= 900/X$$
$$= 20$$
$$X = Rp/Q$$
$$= 900/20$$
$$= 45 \text{ ohms}$$

Now you need to find the inductance of a coil which has a reactance of 45 ohms at the desired frequency (10,000 Hz). The general formula for inductive reactance is;

$$X1 = 2 \pi FL$$

(π is pi, about 3.14.)

In this case, you know X1 is 45, but you do not know the value of L. Therefore, algebraically rearrange the equation;

$$L = X1/(2 \pi F)$$
$$= 45/(2 \times 3.14 \times 10000)$$
$$= 45/62832$$
$$= 0.0007162 \text{ henry}$$
$$= 0.72 \text{ mH}$$
$$= 720 \mu H$$

If you round this off to the more convenient and more readily available value of 750 μH, the actual inductive reactance at 10,000 Hz is approximately;

$$X = 2 \pi FL$$
$$= 2 \times 3.14 \times 10000 \times 0.00075$$
$$= 47 \text{ ohms}$$

This changes the actual Q to;

$$Q = Rp/X$$
$$= 900/47$$
$$= 19.1$$

This is certainly close enough.

At resonance, the capacitive reactance should be equal to the inductive reactance. The formula for finding the capacitive reactance is;

$$Xc = 1/(2 \pi FC)$$

This equation can easily be algebraically rearranged to solve for the desired capacitance from a known capacitive inductance;

$$C = 1/(2 \pi FX_c)$$
$$= 1/(2 \times 3.14 \times 10000 \times 45)$$
$$= 1/2827433$$
$$= 0.00000035 \text{ farad}$$
$$= 0.35 \ \mu F$$

This is the total estimated capacitance in the LC tank; that is, the series combination of C1 and C2. For simplicity, ignore the relatively minor effects of tuning capacitor C3 for the time being.

Now, let's consider the effects of the tuning capacitor C3. This capacitor is used to give a range of user-selectable output frequencies. If a narrow range is desired, especially if C3 is only needed to fine tune the output frequency over a small range, only a small parallel capacitance is needed. For a more extensive range of frequencies, a larger variable capacitor can be used.

Let's assume that C3 is a 365 pF (0.000000000365 farad) tuning capacitor. This value was selected because it is very widely available. It is the size often used to tune portable AM radios. Also assume that at its minimum setting, its capacitance is 5 pF (0.000000000005 farad).

You already know that the series combination of C1 and C2 is 0.35 μF (0.00000035 farad). This combined value is called Cs. This allows us to simplify the equation for the parallel combination to:

$$C_t = C_3 + C_s$$

When C3 is at its minimum setting, its effect on the total capacitance is negligible:

$$C_t = 0.000005 + 0.35$$
$$= 0.350005 \ \mu F$$

The output frequency (resonance) at this setting is;

$$F_h = 1/(2 \pi \sqrt{LC_t})$$
$$= 1/(2 \times 3.14 \times \sqrt{(0.00075 \times 0.000000350005)} \ )$$
$$= 1/(6.28 \times \sqrt{0.00000000026250375})$$
$$= 1/(6.28 \times 0.0000162)$$

$$= 1/0.0001018$$
$$= 9823 \text{ Hz}$$

This is a little lower than the target frequency of 10,000 Hz, but it is the highest frequency that will be generated by the circuit. If this was a critical application, you would need to go back and select new values for L1, C1, and C2 to correct for the cumulative rounding errors. For now, assume that the application isn't all that critical, so 9823 Hz is close enough.

Now, consider what happens when C3 is set to its maximum value. The total tank capacitance is now;

$$Ct = 0.000365 + 0.35$$
$$= 0.350365 \ \mu\text{F}$$

This makes the resonant frequency equal to;

$$F1 = 1/(2 \times 3.14 \times \sqrt{(0.00075 \times 0.000000350365)})$$
$$= 1/(6.28 \times \sqrt{0.0000000002652375})$$
$$= 1/(6.28 \times 0.0000163)$$
$$= 1/0.0001023$$
$$= 9772.5 \text{ Hz}$$

Because C3's maximum value is relatively small with respect to Cs (the series combination of C1 and C2), the range of output frequencies is rather small. The output frequency with the component values listed in this discussion can range from 9772.5 Hz to 9823 Hz. This is a total range of just 50.5 Hz, which is suitable for fine-tuning. If you want an oscillator that can cover a wider range of output frequencies, you will need to increase the maximum value of C3.

For large output frequency ranges, select a large value for parallel tuning capacitor for C3. For small, fine-tuning output ranges, use a relatively small value for parallel tuning capacitor C3.

Capacitors C1 and C2 function as a voltage divider, as discussed earlier in this section. If they are equal, half of the power within the LC trap reaches the transistor's emitter through ground.

In a practical design, you will usually want to limit the amount of this feedback. If there is too much feedback, the repeated reamplification causes the transistor to try to put a voltage greater than its source voltage. Clearly, this is impossible. The signal will be clipped and badly distorted. In addition, some transistors may build up excessive heat if overdriven like this for an extended period of time. This excessive heat could cause the delicate semiconductor crystal to self-destruct.

The feedback can be limited somewhat by placing a resistor (R3) between the emitter and ground, as shown in the diagram. A capacitor (C5) in parallel with this emitter resistor improves circuit stability.

The voltage gain is equal to;

$$Av = B \times (R1/Zi)$$

where R1 is the load resistance, Zi is the input impedance of the transistor, and B is the transistor's beta value.

R1 is approximately 900 ohms, and you can get the beta from the specification sheet for the transistor. For the HEP-50, B is 85.

The approximate formula for the input impedance is;

$$Zi = B \times (26/1c)$$

The maximum current drawn by the amplifier stage is;

$$
\begin{aligned}
Ic &= Vcc/R1 \\
&= 9/900 \\
&= 0.01 \text{ ampere} \\
&= 10 \text{ mA}
\end{aligned}
$$

Since the quiescent operating point should be half the maximum range you can assign a value of 5 mA to Ic. This makes the input impedance equal to about;

$$
\begin{aligned}
Zi &= 85 \times (26/5) \\
&= 85 \times 5.2 \\
&= 442 \text{ ohms}
\end{aligned}
$$

Now you have enough information to solve for the voltage gain of the amplifier stage;

$$
\begin{aligned}
Av &= B \times (R1/Zi) \\
&= 85 \times 900/442 \\
&= 85 \times 2.04 \\
&= 173
\end{aligned}
$$

A good rule of thumb in designing oscillators is to divide this value by about 4, and round the result off to a convenient value. In the sample design, this gives a desired voltage gain of;

$$Ava = Av/4$$
$$= 173/4$$
$$= 43.25$$

This can be rounded off to 45.

If C1 and C2 are of equal value, they divide this gain factor in half, giving an effective gain of 22.5. For maximum stability, however, the gain should be only slightly better than unity (a little greater than 1).

For the best stability (and most efficient power output), you'll also want matched impedances. The capacitive divider is used to achieve both of these goals. Once you have adjusted the C1/C2 ratio for the best impedance matching, you can trim the gain by adjusting the value of emitter resistor R3.

The desired value for C2 can be calculated with this formula;

$$C2 = Ct \sqrt{Ro/Ri}$$

where Ct is the total value of the C1-C2 series combination (0.35 μF in our example problem). Ro is the output impedance/resistance. It is assumed to be the same as R1 (900 ohms). Ri is the input impedance/resistance, and has the same value as Zi (442 ohms). So, for the sample design, C2 should be equal to;

$$C2 = 0.35 \times \sqrt{900/442}$$
$$= 0.35 \times \sqrt{2.04}$$
$$= 0.35 \times 1.43$$
$$= 0.5 \ \mu F$$

Now just rearrange the series combination equation to find the necessary value for C1;

$$1/Ct = 1/C1 + 1/C2$$
$$1/C1 = 1/Ct - 1/C2$$
$$= 1/0.35 - 1/0.5$$
$$= 2.857 - 2$$

$$1/C1 = 0.857$$
$$C1 = 1.17 \ \mu F$$

This can be rounded off to 1.2 μF.

You have completed most of the design now. There are just a few component values still needed to complete the circuit.

First, the emitter resistor (R3) is selected to give the desired gain. One method of determining the value for this resistor is to breadboard the circuit using a trimpot in place of R3. Monitor the oscillator's output with an oscilloscope and adjust R3's value for the cleanest possible output waveform. Then replace the trimpot with a fixed resistor whose value is equal to the setting of the trimpot.

You can also approximate the value for this resistor by using a simple gain equation often used in designing amplifiers;

$$Av = Rcc/Re$$

The problem with this approach is that Rcc is made up of the reactances of several separate components. This makes the actual calculations very complex. The experimental method is usually more convenient and practical.

If you do not have an oscilloscope handy, R3's value can be experimentally adjusted by running the output through an amplifier and speaker. Just adjust the trimpot for the strongest, purest tone. There should be no raspiness in the tone at all.

This emitter resistor usually has a very small value, in the 50 to 200 ohm range.

Capacitor C4 should be selected so that its reactance at the resonant frequency is about one tenth of the nominal load resistance (R1):

$$
\begin{aligned}
Xc4 &= R1/10 \\
&= 900/10 \\
&= 90 \\
C4 &= 1/2 \ F \times c4 \\
&= 1/(2 \times 3.14 \times 10000 \times 90) \\
&= 1/5654867 \\
&= 0.00000018 \ \text{farad} \\
&= 0.18 \ \mu F
\end{aligned}
$$

You can round this value off and use a standard 0.2 μF or 0.22 μF

capacitor. These equations are only approximations. The exact values are not very critical.

Coil L2 serves as a choke. To prevent its dc resistance from limiting the output of the oscillator, this coil should have a high reactance compared to the load resistance (R1). As a rule of thumb, the inductive reactance of L2 at the output frequency should be at least 50 times greater than the nominal load resistance;

$$
\begin{aligned}
X12 &= 50 \times R1 \\
&= 50 \times 900 \\
&= 45000 \text{ ohms}
\end{aligned}
$$

This equation gives a minimum value. Let's boost it up a little, and round it off to 50,000 ohms.

Again you can find the inductance from the inductive reactance by algebraically rearranging the standard formula for inductive reactance;

$$
\begin{aligned}
L &= X1/(2\pi F) \\
&= 50000/(2 \times 3.14 \times 10000) \\
&= 50000/62832 \\
&= 0.796 \text{ henry} \\
&= 800 \text{ mH}
\end{aligned}
$$

Capacitor C5 normally has a value equal to that of C4, which is 0.2 μF in our sample design.

Resistor R2 should have a value approximately 5 times that of R3;

$$
R2 = 5R3
$$

Finally, the formula for R1 is:

$$
R1 = ((R2 \times Vcc)/Ve) - R2
$$

Ve is the voltage drop across R3. Ohm's law lets you find that value:

$$
Ve = IeR3
$$

And since the emitter current is roughly equal to the collector current, this can be rewritten as;

$$
Ve = IcR3
$$

which is handy, since 1c was already found in one of the earlier equations.

Assuming a value of 100 ohms for R3, the other two resistances work out to;

$$R2 = 5 \times 100$$
$$= 500 \text{ ohms}$$
$$= 470 \text{ ohms}$$

$$Ve = 0.005 \times 100$$
$$= 0.5 \text{ volt}$$

$$R1 = ((470 \times 9)/0.5) - 470$$
$$= (4230/0.5) - 470$$
$$= 8460 - 470$$
$$= 7990$$
$$= 8200 \text{ ohms } (8.2k)$$

All of the calculated parts values for this sample Colpitts oscillator are listed in Table 2-2.

As might be expected with any popular circuit, there are a number of variations on the basic Colpitts oscillator. One frequently encountered variant is the Ultra-Audion oscillator, shown in Fig. 2-9. This circuit is very well suited for vhf (very high frequency) applications. It is often used as the local oscillator for television tuners.

Internal capacitances within the transistor itself provide the feedback paths at vhf frequencies. These internal capacitances function as if they were small external capacitors connected from the base to the emitter, and from the emitter to the collector. These internal capacitances have a very low reactance in the vhf range.

Table 2-2. Typical Parts List for the Colpitts Oscillator Project (Fig. 2-8).

Q1	almost any NPN transistor (2N3904, 2N2222, etc.)
L1	0.1 μH coil
C1	365 pF variable capacitor
C2, C4, C5	0.1 μF capacitor*
C3	0.2 μF capacitor*
R1, R2	1000 ohms (minimum)**

*	experiment with other values for C2 and C3
**	experiment with other resistance values greater than 1000 ohms

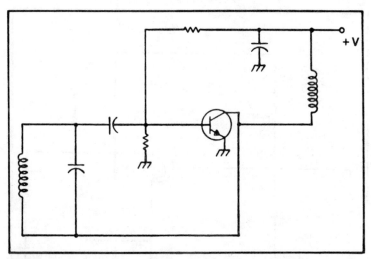

Fig. 2-9. The ultra-audion oscillator is a popular variation on the basic Colpitts oscillator.

The Ultra-Audion oscillator can also be used at lower frequencies, but larger external capacitors need to be added to the circuit, as illustrated in Fig. 2-10.

Another variation on the basic Colpitts oscillator is the Clapp oscillator, shown in Fig. 2-11. The Clapp oscillator is rather unique in that it is tuned by a series resonant LC tank, rather than the more common parallel resonant LC tank. Feedback for the Clapp

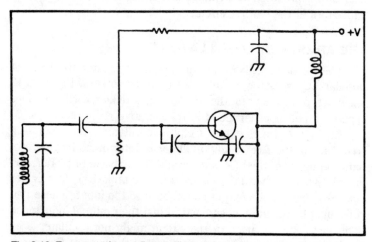

Fig. 2-10. To use an ultra-audion oscillator at lower frequencies, larger external capacitors must be added to the circuit.

51

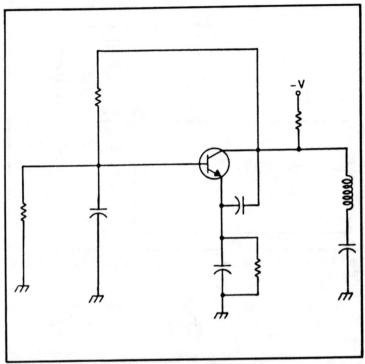

Fig. 2-11. The Clapp oscillator is unique in that it uses a series resonant LC tank for tuning.

oscillator is provided by a voltage divider formed by the two small capacitors in the emitter circuit.

THE ARMSTRONG OSCILLATOR

The Hartley oscillator and the Colpitts oscillator are the most popular LC oscillator circuits, but there are others. Figure 2-12 shows a typical circuit for the Armstrong, or tickler, oscillator. This type of circuit is often found in regenerative radio receivers.

As in the Hartley and Colpitts oscillators, the operating frequency of the Armstrong oscillator is determined by the resonant frequency of the LC Tank circuit. A feedback, or tickler, coil is closely coupled with the main coil of the tank (L1). The tickler coil feeds part of the output signal back to the input. These two coils must be carefully positioned so that their mutual inductance is of the proper polarity, or the circuit might not oscillate.

Potentiometer R3 controls the level of the current flowing in the tickler coil, and thus, the amount of feedback or regeneration.

THE TITO OSCILLATOR

Another type of LC oscillator circuit is the Tuned-Input/Tuned-Output, or TITO, oscillator. Often, if the circuit is designed around a tube, it is called the Tuned-Grid/Tuned-Plate (TGTP) oscillator. The transistor version is often called the Tuned-Base/Tuned-Collector oscillator.

The basic TITO circuit is illustrated in Fig. 2-13. This circuit is rather unique, in that it has two LC tanks. Both play a part in determining the frequency of oscillations. As a rule, the circuit functions best when the two tanks are resonant at different, but nearly equal, frequencies.

Inter-element capacitances within the transistor (or tube) itself provides the feedback path in the TITO oscillator. Capacitors Cbe

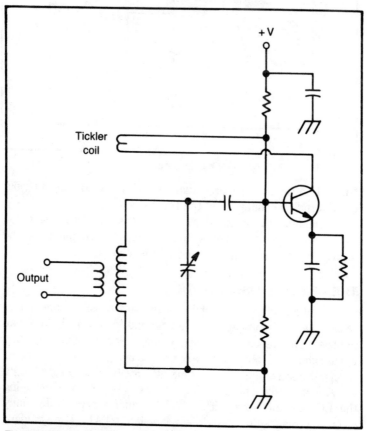

Fig. 2-12. The Armstrong oscillator is often employed in regenerative radio receiver circuits.

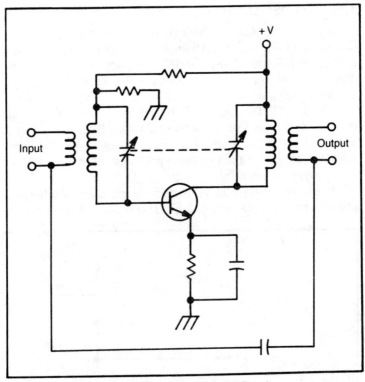

Fig. 2-13. The TITO oscillator has two separate LC tanks.

and Ccb in the diagram are usually not discrete components, but the internal capacitances of the transistor.

Although it's interesting, the TITO oscillator isn't too commonly employed today. A similar type of circuit appears as the local oscillators in some TV and FM receivers.

THE CRYSTAL OSCILLATOR

A coil and capacitor tank is not the only possible approach to resonance. Coil and capacitor values tend to be a little less than precise. The resonant frequency may tend to drift in some circumstances. Often, this type of error is insignificant, but in some precision applications, the LC tank may not be quite good enough.

A more precise resonant frequency can be set-up by replacing the LC tank network with a slab of quartz crystal. In many electronic diagrams, crystals are labelled XTAL. The standard schematic symbol for a crystal is shown in Fig. 2-14.

The basic structure of a crystal is illustrated in Fig. 2-15. A

54

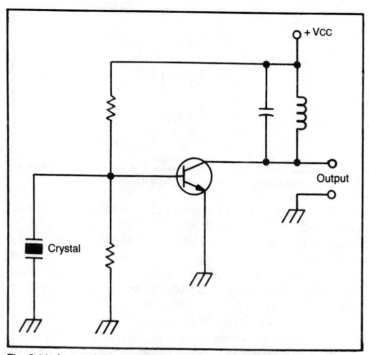

Fig. 2-14. A crystal can be used in the place of a resonant LC tank.

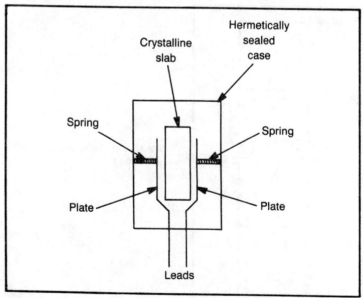

Fig. 2-15. The crystal's internal structure is delicate, but not overly complicated.

55

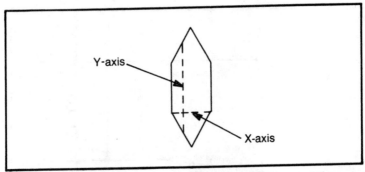

Fig. 2-16. A crystal has two sets of perpendicular axes.

thin slice of quartz crystal is sandwiched between two metallic plates, which are held in tight contact with the crystalline slab by small springs. This entire assembly is enclosed in a hermetically sealed metal case. The hermetic seal helps keep out any contamination, such as moisture and dust. Leads connected to the metal endplates are brought out from the case to permit connection to an external circuitry.

A crystal works because of a phenomenon known as the piezoelectric effect. Two sets of axes pass through the body of the crystal. One set, called the X axis, passes through the corners of

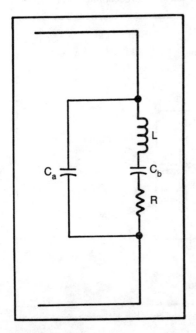

Fig. 2-17. The equivalent circuit for a typical crystal.

the crystal. The other set, called the Y axis, lies perpendicular to the X axis, but in the same plane, as illustrated in Fig. 2-16. Practical crystals are made of a very thin slice of crystalline material. This slice may be cut across either an X axis or a Y axis.

If a mechanical stress is placed across the Y axis, an electrical voltage is produced along the X axis. Similarly, if an electrical voltage is applied across the X axis, a mechanical stress appears along the Y axis. This is the piezoelectric effect. The piezoelectric effect can cause the crystal to ring (vibrate) or resonant at a specific frequency under certain conditions.

Electrically, a crystal functions like the simple circuit shown in Fig. 2-17. Depending on how the crystal is manufactured, it may resemble either a series-resonant or a parallel-resonant LC tank. Generally speaking, a crystal designed for series-resonant use can not be used in a parallel-resonant circuit.

The resonant frequency of a crystal is determined primarily by the thickness and size of the crystal slice. Crystals can also be

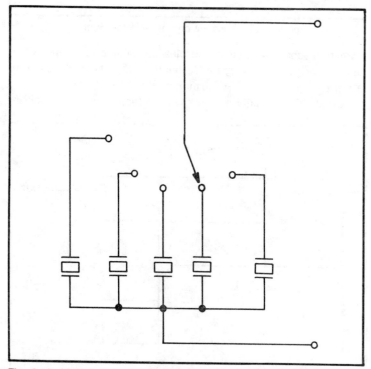

Fig. 2-18. Multiple crystals may be wired in parallel and selected by a multiposition switch.

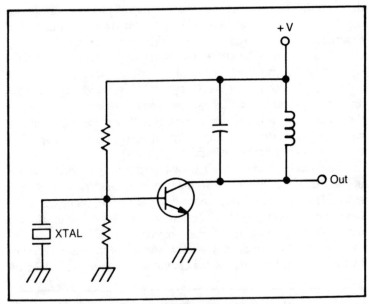

Fig. 2-19. A typical parallel resonant crystal oscillator circuit.

made to resonant at integer multiples (harmonics) of its main resonant frequency; however, the resonance effect becomes steadily less pronounced at higher harmonics.

Crystals are usually more expensive than separate capacitors

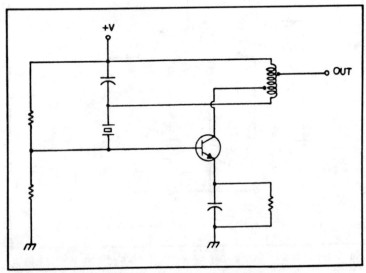

Fig. 2-20. A typical series resonant crystal oscillator circuit.

and coils. Also it is not easy to alter the resonant frequency in a crystal based circuit. On the other hand, LC resonant circuits often drift off frequency (that is, the frequency-determining components change their values slightly), particularly under changing temperature conditions.

Crystals are also somewhat temperature sensitive, although not as much so as capacitors and coils. When extremely high accuracy is required (as in broadcasting applications, for example), a crystal oscillator circuit is enclosed in a special crystal oven, which maintains a constant temperature for the crystal.

Reliability is another major advantage for crystals. The failure rate for crystals tends to be significantly lower than for capacitors and coils. However, a crystal can be damaged by high over-voltages, or extremely high temperatures. A severe mechanical shock (such as being dropped onto a hard surface) can crack the delicate crystal slab.

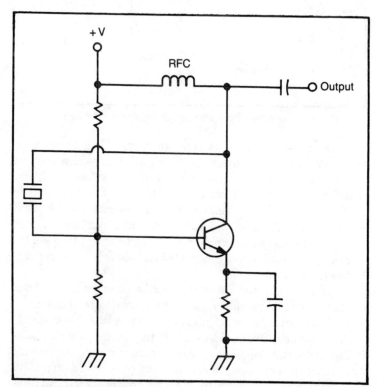

Fig. 2-21. The Pierce oscillator is a popular variation on the basic crystal oscillator circuit.

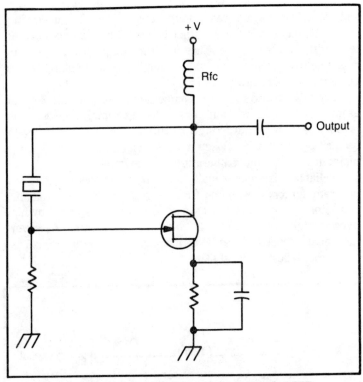

Fig. 2-22. Pierce oscillators can also be constructed around FETs.

The most important disadvantage of crystals is the same as their most important advantage. The resonant frequency of the crystal is inherent in its manufacture, and is a constant. The resonant frequency generally can't be changed. In a LC circuit, one or both of the frequency determining components can be made variable. But there is no such thing as a variable crystal. Occasionally, special external circuitry can be added for a limited degree of fine tuning, but this limited technique is the exception, rather than the rule.

The only way the frequency can be changed in a crystal oscillator is to physically replace the crystal. For this reason, crystals are usually inserted into sockets, rather than permanently soldered into the circuit. The leads of the crystal plug into holes in a special socket which makes electrical contact with the external circuit. Crystals can easily and quickly be removed and replaced. Using sockets also sidesteps the potential problem of thermal damage resulting from soldering the crystal's leads directly.

In some circuits, multiple crystals may be wired in parallel, and selected by a multiposition switch, as illustrated in Fig. 2-18.

A typical crystal oscillator circuit is shown in Fig. 2-19. In this circuit, the crystal is operated in the parallel-resonant mode.

A typical series-resonant crystal oscillator is illustrated in Fig. 2-20.

The Pierce oscillator is a popular variation on the basic crystal oscillator. The crystal is connected between the base and the collector of the transistor, as shown in Fig. 2-21. If a FET is used, the crystal is placed between the gate and drain leads, as shown in Fig. 2-22. In the Pierce oscillator, the crystal acts as its own tuned circuit, eliminating the need for an adjustable LC tank in the output. Pierce oscillator circuits are frequently employed in rf (radio frequency) applications.

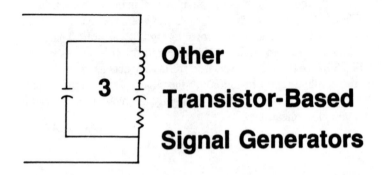

3

Other Transistor-Based Signal Generators

THE SINE WAVE IS NOT THE ONLY USEFUL WAVEFORM. IN many applications, more complex waveforms are much more useful than the simple sine wave. Theoretically, complex waveforms can be synthesized by combining multiple sine waves of the proper frequencies and phase relationships. However, this technique, which is known as additive synthesis, is rarely very practical in real world applications.

This chapter examines a number of fairly simple transistor circuits that generate common, moderately complex waveforms, such as triangle waves, rectangle waves, and sawtooth waves.

TRIANGLE WAVE GENERATORS

Most triangle wave generators are based on the charging and discharging of a capacitor. A practical triangle wave generator circuit is illustrated in Fig. 3-1. A typical parts list for this circuit is given in Table 3-1.

Capacitor C1 has a major effect on the output frequency. Potentiometer R3 functions as a fine tuning control. This circuit can be used over a wide range of frequencies, simply by selecting a suitable value for C1. The larger the capacitance of C1, the lower the output frequency is. Depending on the value of C1, this circuit can generate frequencies as low as a few hertz, up to several Megahertz (millions of hertz). Frequency ranges for several typical values of C1 are listed in Table 3-2.

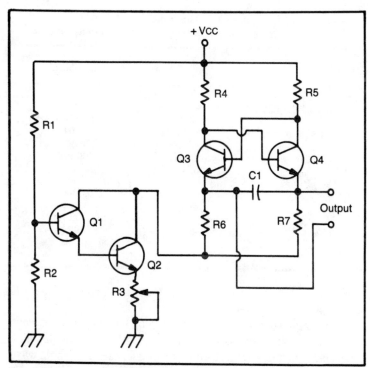

Fig. 3-1. A practical circuit for generating triangle waves.

Actually, this circuit does not really generate the triangle wave directly. Transistors Q3 and Q4, and their associated components, make up an astable multivibrator, or square wave generator. (This basic configuration also appears in the rectangle wave circuits described in the next section.) The square wave is shaped into a triangle wave by Q1 and Q2. A square wave at the same frequency as the triangle wave can be tapped off from the collector of either

Table 3-1. Typical Parts List for the
Triangle Wave Generator Circuit of Fig. 3-1.

Q1,Q2,Q3,Q4	2N3648 NPN transistor (or similar)
R1	18K (18,000 ohms)
R2	4.2K (4200 ohms)
R3	1K potentiometer
R4,R5	330 ohm
R6,R7	4.7K (4700 ohms)
C1	see text
V_{cc}	12 volts

C1	MINIMUM	MAXIMUM
100 pF (0.0001 μF)	5.6 MHz (5,600,000 Hz)	10 MHz (10,000,000 Hz)
1000 pF (0.001 μF)	560 kHz (560,000 Hz)	1 MHz (1,000,000 Hz)
0.01 μF	56 kHz (56,000 Hz)	100 kHz (100,000 Hz)
0.1 μF	5.6 khz (5,600 Hz)	10 kHz (10,000 Hz)
1 μF	560 Hz	1 kHz (1,000 Hz)
10 μF	56 Hz	100 Hz
100 μF	5.6 Hz	10 Hz

transistor Q3, or Q4. The signals at these two collectors are 180 out of phase with each other.

A triangle wave can also be created by feeding a square wave signal through a low-pass filter. A low-pass filter attenuates high frequencies, but doesn't disturb lower frequencies. A triangle wave has the same harmonic content as a square wave, but the harmonic amplitudes are weaker in the triangle signal.

RECTANGLE WAVE GENERATORS

Probably the most common waveform in modern electronics is the rectangle wave (and its specific variations, the square wave and the pulse wave). Rectangle waves are used in both digital and analog applications.

A rectangle wave is made up of just two discrete levels: a low level and a high level. An ideal rectangle wave switches instantly from one level to the other with zero transition time. Practical rectangle waves always have some finite transition time between states, although it is often negligible for most applications.

There are many varieties of rectangle waves, distinguished by their duty cycles, the ratio between the high level (on) time and the complete cycle time. In a square wave, the signal is high for exactly one half of each cycle, and low for the other half. This means the duty cycle is 1:2. In a pulse wave, the high level time makes up only a very small portion of the entire cycle. For most of the

64

cycle, the signal is at its low level. A rectangle wave may have any duty cycle. Square waves and pulse waves are simply special cases of the rectangle wave.

To generate a rectangle wave, you have to be able to switch quickly between the two output levels. A transistor can function as a high-speed electronic switch, so it is suitable for rectangle wave generation. This section looks at just a few typical transistor-based rectangle wave generator circuits.

A super-simple rectangle wave generator circuit is shown in Fig. 3-2. Almost any general purpose NPN transistors can be used in this circuit, but both should be of the same type number. When power is applied to this circuit, one of the two transistors starts to conduct slightly faster than its partner, since no two transistors are ever exactly identical. Let's say that Q1 conducts a little more heavily than Q2. Q2 is cut off because Q1's collector voltage is applied to the base of Q2. But, as Q1 continues to conduct more heavily, the collector voltage starts to drop. At some point, the base of Q2 is at a voltage that allows this transistor to turn on and start conducting. When conduction begins, the collector voltage of Q2

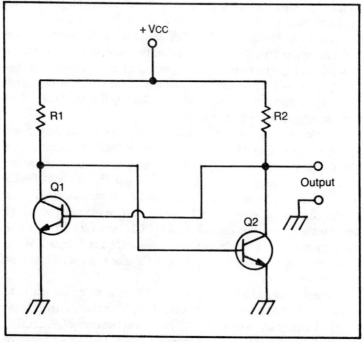

Fig. 3-2. A quick & dirty rectangle wave generator circuit.

is very high. This voltage is fed to the base of Q1, cutting the first transistor off.

The two transistors switch back and forth in this fashion, turning each other on and off for as long as power is applied to the circuit. If you tap off a signal from one of the transistor's collectors, you will get a rectangle wave. In the diagram, the output is tapped off from the collector of Q2. The signal at the collector of Q1 could also be used. The two collector signals are 180 degrees out of phase with each other.

The speed of the switching (and thus, the output frequency) is determined by the two collector resistors (the only other components in the circuit). If these two resistors have equal values, each transistor is on for an equal length of time, and the output is a square wave. Rectangle waves with other duty cycles can easily be achieved just by using unequal resistances. For reliable performance, the resistance values should be kept between 100 ohms and 2.2 k (2,200 ohms).

Obviously, being made up of just four components, this is about the simplest rectangle wave generator circuit you are likely to find. Of course, it is not terribly precise either in terms of output frequency or waveshape but it is perfectly adequate for non-critical applications.

A somewhat more sophisticated variation on this simple circuit is illustrated in Fig. 3-3. In this circuit, the individual transistor on times (and therefore the output frequency) is determined by the charging rates of the capacitors, along with the circuit resistances. Once again, equal component values in the two halves of the circuit yield a square wave at the output.

The circuit shown in Fig. 3-4 is even more sophisticated and precise, at the expense of an increased component count. This circuit can be employed over a wide range of output frequencies. Reasonably clean rectangle waves from 0.5 Hz to about 60 Hz (60,000 Hz) can be produced by this circuit. A standardized parts list for this circuit is given in Table 3-3. Three component values are omitted from the parts list: R11, C1, and C2. These three component values are selected for the desired output signal. Before calculating these component values, let's take a quick look at how this circuit works.

When power is applied to the circuit, transistor Q1 starts to conduct. The collector voltage of this transistor rises, charging capacitor C2 through resistor R4. This cuts off transistor Q2, causing its collector voltage to become more negative. This puts a negative

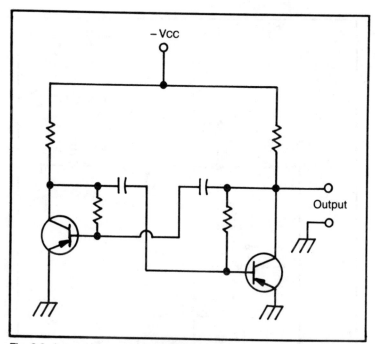

Fig. 3-3. A somewhat more sophisticated rectangle wave generator circuit.

charge across capacitor C1, speeding up the on time of transistor Q3.

Before long, the charge across capacitor C2 is equal to 63% of the supply voltage (VCC). At this point, the capacitor starts to discharge through Q1, which exhibits a low impedance. Now the second half of the cycle begins, with transistors Q1 and Q2 trading roles, and capacitor C1 becoming charged through resistor R3.

The value of resistor R11 is dependent on the load being used for the specific intended application. The formula is:

$$R11 = V_o/I_{c3max} \times I_l$$

where V_o is the output voltage, I_{c3max} is the maximum collector current of transistor Q3, and I_l is the load current. If a 12 volt supply voltage is used for VCC. V_o should be no more than I_l volts.

The output frequency is determined by capacitors C1 and C2. The formula for C1 is:

$$C1 = (I_{cl} \times Tl)/(0.63 \ VCC)$$

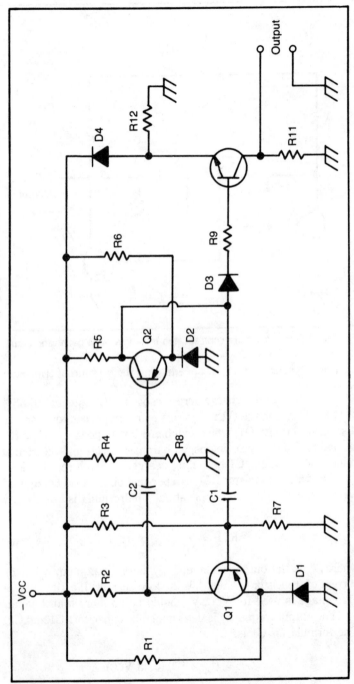

Fig. 3-4. For more precise applications, this deluxe rectangle wave generator circuit can be used.

68

Q1, Q2	PNP transistor (2N1303 or similar)
Q3	NPN transistor (2N1302 or similar)
D1, D2	1N463 diode
D3	1N95 diode
D4	1N645 diode
C1	see text
C2	see text
R1, R6	12 k resistor
R2	360 ohm, 1 watt resistor
R3, R4	3.6 k resistor
R5	910 ohm resistor
R7, R8	620 ohm resistor
R9	510 ohm resistor
R10	100 ohm resistor
R11	see text
R12	5.6 k resistor
Vcc	− 12 volts

where I_{c1} is the collector current of transistor Q1, and Tl is the time (in seconds) then the output signal is to be in its low state in a single cycle. VCC, of course, is the circuit's supply voltage.

The equation for C2 is similar:

$$C2 = (Ic2 \times Th)/(0.63\ VCC)$$

This time the collector current of transistor Q2 (Ic2) and the length (in seconds) of the high level time per second is used.

Clearly, the total length of a single cycle is the sum of the low and high times:

$$Tt = Tl + Th$$

The frequency is simply the reciprocal of the cycle time:

$$F = 1/Tt$$
$$= 1/(Tl = Th)$$

Rearranging and combining these equations, we find:

$$Tl = (0.63\ VCCC1)/Icl$$
$$Th = (0.63\ VCCC2)/Ic2$$
$$Tt = [(0.63\ VCCC1)/Icl] + [(0.63\ VCCC2)/Ic2]$$
$$F = I/\{[(0.63\ VCCC1)/Icl] + [(0.63\ VCCC2)/Ic2]\}$$

You can simplify these equations somewhat by deciding on and plugging in specific standard values wherever possible. VCC is defined in the parts list as 12 volts. Typical values for the two collector currents (which are nearly equal in almost all cases) are approximately 0.03 ampere (30 mA). Plugging these values into our equations, we get:

$$
\begin{aligned}
Tl &= (0.63 \times 12 \times C1)/0.03 \\
&= 7.56C1/0.03 \\
&= 252C1 \\
Th &= (0.63 \times 12 \times c2)/0.03 \\
&= 7.56C2/0.03 \\
&= 252C2 \\
Tt &= 252C1 + 252C2 \\
&= 252(C1 + C2) \\
F &= 1/[252(C1 + C2)]
\end{aligned}
$$

This is certainly a significant improvement!

For a square wave, things get even simpler. By definition, a square wave has equal high and low times. That is:

$$Tl = Th$$

Therefore:

$$
\begin{aligned}
252C1 &= 252C2 \\
C1 &= C2 = C \\
Tt &= 252(C + C) \\
&= 252 \times 2 \times C \\
&= 504C \\
F &= 1/504C
\end{aligned}
$$

Let's say that you want a square wave with a frequency of 1000 Hz. The first step is to algebraically rearrange the frequency equation:

$$C = 1/504F$$

Then simply solve for C, since the same value is used for both C1 and C2:

$$C = 1(504 \times 1000)$$

$$= 1/504000$$
$$= 0.000002 \text{ farad}$$
$$= 2 \ \mu F$$

And that's all there is to that.

For other duty cycles, the design procedure is only slightly more complicated. Let's assume you need to generate a 12 kHz (12,000 Hz) rectangle wave with a duty cycle of 1:5. First, simply take the reciprocal of the desired frequency to find the total cycle time:

$$Tt = 1/F$$
$$= 1/12000$$
$$= 0.0000833 \text{ second}$$

To achieve the desired duty cycle, the high time should be equal to 1/5 of the total cycle time:

$$Th = 1/5 \times Tt$$
$$= 0.0000833/5$$
$$= 0.0000167 \text{ second}$$

Now, simple subtraction can give us the appropriate low time:

$$Tl = Tt - Th$$
$$= 0.0000833 - 0.0000167$$
$$= 0.0000666 \text{ second}$$

Earlier you learned that:

$$Tl = 252C1$$

We can rearrange this equation to find a suitable value for C1:

$$C1 = Tl/252$$
$$= 0.0000666/252$$
$$= 0.00000026 \text{ farad}$$
$$= 0.26 \ \mu F$$

Similarly, solving for C2:

$$C2 = Th/252$$
$$= 0.0000167/252$$

$$= \quad 0.0000000663 \text{ farad}$$
$$= \quad 0.0663 \ \mu\text{F}$$

For convenience, you can round the capacitances off to the nearest standard capacitor values; probably a 0.27 μF capacitor for C1, and a 0.068 μF capacitor for C2.

Double-check your work, and see how much the rounding off has affected the output frequency. Remember, you were shooting for an output frequency of 12,000 Hz:

$$
\begin{aligned}
F \ & = \ 1/[252(C1 + C2)] \\
& = \ 1/[252(0.00000027 + 0.000000068)] \\
& = \ 1/(252 \times 0.000000338) \\
& = \ 1/0.000085176 \\
& = \ 11740 \text{ Hz}
\end{aligned}
$$

There is a 260 Hz error stemming from the cumulative effects of rounding off values in the various calculations. This degree of error isn't too bad; it is only 2.2% off, close enough for all but the most critical applications.

Let's try one more example before moving on. This time, we generate a 4300 Hz rectangle wave with a duty cycle of 1:3. Working through the various equations as before, you'll come up with the following results:

$$
\begin{aligned}
Tt \ & = \ 1/F \\
& = \ 1/4300 \\
& = \ 0.0002326 \text{ second} \\
Th \ & = \ Tt/3 \\
& = \ 0.000236/3 \\
& = \ 0.0000775 \text{ second} \\
Tl \ & = \ Tt - Th \\
& = \ 0.0002326 - 0.0000775 \\
& = \ 0.0001551 \text{ second} \\
C1 \ & = \ Tl/252 \\
& = \ 0.0001551/151 \\
& = \ 0.00000062 \text{ farad} \\
& = \ 0.62 \ \mu\text{F} \\
C2 \ & = \ Tl/252 \\
& = \ 0.0000775/252 \\
& = \ 0.00000031 \text{ farad} \\
& = \ 0.31 \ \mu\text{F}
\end{aligned}
$$

C2 can be rounded off to 0.33 μF.

To double-check the results, recalculate the frequency:

$$
\begin{aligned}
F &= 1/(252(C1 + C2)) \\
&= 1/[252(0.00000062 + 0.00000033)] \\
&= 1/(252 \times 0.00000095) \\
&= 1/0.0002394 \\
&= 4177 \text{ Hz}
\end{aligned}
$$

This is 97.1% of the desired output frequency of 4300 Hz.

As you can see, it is not difficult to come close to the desired output frequency with a minimum of mathematical equations. If greater precision is required for a specific application, you can replace resistors R3 and R4 with trimpots to fine tune the output frequency.

I suggest using a 2.2 k resistor in series with a 2.5 trimpot for each of these resistors. Calculate the nominal values for C1 and C2 in the usual manner. Then construct (or breadboard) the circuit and adjust the trimpots while monitoring the output signal with a frequency counter or oscilloscope.

There is one major disadvantage to this method: the two controls interact, affecting both the output frequency and the duty cycle. This fine-tuning procedure requires patience.

A rather novel rectangle wave generator is shown in Fig. 3-5. This circuit offers three related outputs. Some typical signals generated by this circuit are illustrated in Fig. 3-6. This type of circuit is very useful for sequential switching, especially at fairly low frequencies. Additional stages can easily be added, if desired.

The three output pulses have equal times when the following conditions are true:

$$
\begin{aligned}
R1 &= R3 = R5 \\
R2 &= R4 = R6 \\
C1 &= C2 = C3
\end{aligned}
$$

The circuit works if these equalities are not true, but the outputs are not symmetrical. I strongly recommend that you try breadboarding this circuit and experiment with various component values.

Almost any general purpose NPN transistor can be used in this circuit. For the best results, all of the transistors in the circuit should be the same type. A good choice would be the 2N3904. A suitable supply voltage is 9 volts.

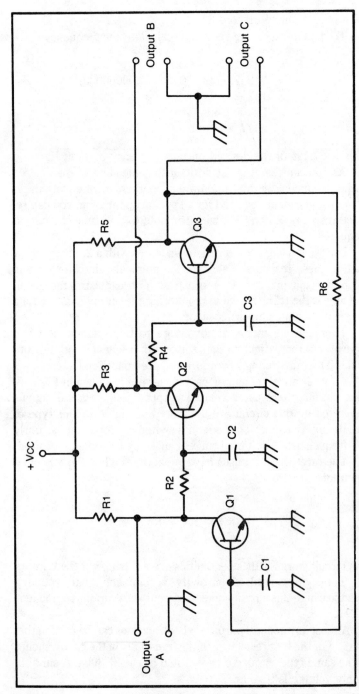

Fig. 3-5. This circuit is a rather novel rectangle wave generator.

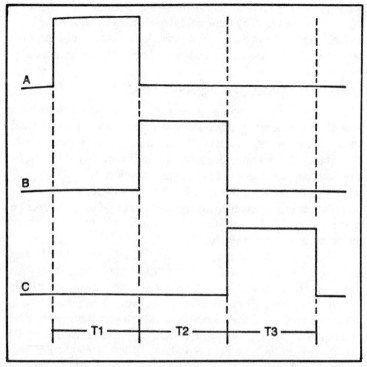

Fig. 3-6. Here are some typical output signals from the circuit of Fig. 3-5.

No parts list is given for this project, because all of the other components in the circuit have a direct effect on the output signal(s), and should be selected for the desired application.

While this circuit is pretty tolerant of almost any component values, it is probably a good idea to stay within the following ranges when experimenting with the circuit:

R1, R3, R5	470 ohms to 3.3 k
R2, R4, R6	10 k to 51 k
C1, C2, C3	0.01 μF to 5 μF

Time Tl is determined by R1, R2, and C1. Similarly, time T2 is set by R3, R4, and C2. Finally, R5, R6, and C3 determine time T3. The cycle repeats after T3.

SAWTOOTH WAVE GENERATORS

This chapter discusses sawtooth-wave generators only in

passing. Most practical transistor-based circuits for generating sawtooth waves employ a special type of transistor called the UJT, or UniJunction Transistor. Since this device is the subject of the next chapter, it is more appropriate to discuss these circuits there.

UNUSUAL WAVEFORM GENERATORS

Most electronics applications call for one of the four basic waveshapes: sine wave, triangle wave, rectangle wave, or sawtooth wave. Occasionally, however, more unusual waveforms may be desirable. This section discusses a handful of signal generator circuits that produce various unusual waveforms.

The circuit shown in Fig. 3-7 is a fairly simple one. Its output waveform is intentionally distorted, and rather difficult to describe. If the output of this circuit is fed to a loudspeaker, the sound produced is a piercing squeal.

This is an interesting circuit to experiment with. A wide variety of values can be used for any of the components. There are just a few simple guidelines to follow when experimenting with this circuit. Transistor Q1 can be almost any general purpose NPN device, such as the 2N3904. Transistor Q2 is a complementary PNP unit, such as the 2N3906. The combined series resistance of R1 and R2 should be kept between about 70 k and 150 k. For best results, fixed resistor R1 should be in the 68 k to 100 k range. A 25 k or 50 k potentiometer should be used for R2.

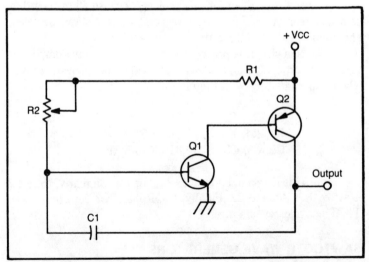

Fig. 3-7. This simple circuit can generate some very complex signals.

The value of capacitor C1 has the most pronounced effect on the output signal. Anything between 0.001 μF and 0.1 μF may be used in this circuit. Several different capacitors can be connected in semi-parallel and selected with a multiposition switch.

> **AN IMPORTANT NOTE:** Some component combinations might draw excessive current through the transistors. If these devices start getting too hot to touch, immediately turn off the power source. Change the resistors/capacitor values, or replace the transistors with similar devices that can safely pass a larger amount of current.

The circuit illustrated in Fig. 3-8 is sort of a double oscillator. By itself, transistor Q2 is a grounded base sine wave oscillator, but at the same time, both of the transistors combine to form a rectangle wave generator. The rectangle wave generator essentially switches the sine wave oscillator's output on and off at a regular rate. The result is a series of pulses, or bursts of a sine wave signal. This combined waveform is shown in Fig. 3-9.

The time determining components for the oscillator's on cycle include C2, R2, D1, and R7. R2 is the primary controlling value for the on time. The off time is set by R3, R4, R7, and C2. R4 is the primary controlling value for the off time. Since the high and low portions of the rectangle wave's cycles are essentially independent, almost any desired duty cycle can be produced by this circuit. However, resistor R2's value tends to interact with the off time. The best procedure is to set the on time first, via R2, then set the off time with R4. The sine wave frequency is set by the resonant frequency of the C5/T1 resonant tank.

A second pulsed generator circuit is shown in Fig. 3-10. This circuit is easier to work with than the previous one. Capacitor C1 determines the main tone frequency, while capacitor C2 determines the pulse switching frequency.

A partial parts list for this circuit is given in Table 3-4. Experiment with various values for the two capacitors. As a rule of thumb, in most applications, C2 should have a much larger value than C1, so that the switching pulse rate is lower than the main tone frequency. Several cycles of the main tone frequency should normally be produced on each pulse.

On the other hand, this is not an absolutely inviolate law. In some applications you may get some very interesting results by

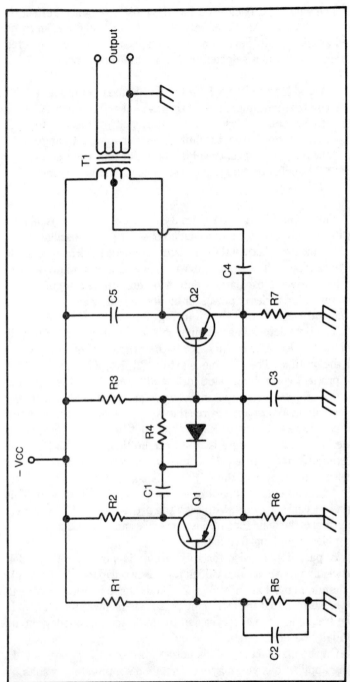

Fig. 3-8. This double oscillator circuit can generate some very unusual waveforms.

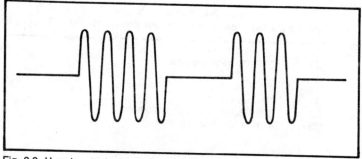

Fig. 3-9. Here is a typical output signal generated by the circuit of Fig. 3-8.

making C1 larger than C2. For the most reliable results, the capacitances should be kept between 0.05 μF and 500 μF. This should be a sufficient range for most applications.

Of course, there are hundreds of other transistor-based signal generator circuits, but this chapter is intended to give you a good basic foundation. Many other circuits are essentially variations of the basic circuits illustrated in this chapter.

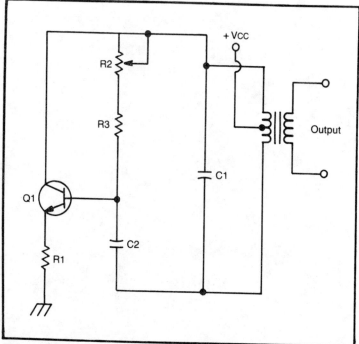

Fig. 3-10. This circuit generates a pulsed signal.

Table 3-4. Partial Parts List
for the Pulsed Waveform Generator Project of Fig. 3-9.

Q1	2N3904 NPN transistor
R1	22 ohm resistor
R2	25K (25,000 ohm) potentiometer
R3	4.7K (4700 ohm) resistor
C1	see text
C2	see text
T1	primary—300 to 1000 ohms secondary—according to output load impedance audio transformer
V_{cc}	9 volt

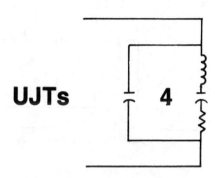

UJTs — 4

NORMALLY, THE TERM "TRANSISTOR" REFERS TO A BIPOLAR transistor. A bipolar transistor is more or less a semiconductor sandwich, as illustrated in Fig. 4-1. There are two types. The NPN transistor is made up of a thin slice of P-type semiconductor between two thicker slabs of N-type semiconductor. The semiconductor types are reversed in the PNP transistor; here we have two thick slabs of P-type semiconductor surrounding a thin slice of N-type semiconductor. Because these devices have two PN junctions, they are called bipolar transistors.

But there are other types of transistors. One of particular importance for signal generator circuits is the UniJunction Transistor, or UJT. This type of transistor has just a single PN junction. The internal structure of an N-type UJT is shown in Fig. 4-2. The standard schematic symbol for this device is illustrated in Fig. 4-3.

P-type UniJunction Transistors also exist. The N-type and P-type sections are simply reversed, as shown in Fig. 4-4. The schematic symbol for a P-type UJT is shown in Fig. 4-5.

For simplicity, this discussion concentrates on the N-type UJT. This information also applies for the P-type UJT, but all polarities are reversed.

HOW A UJT WORKS

The UJT, like the more familiar bipolar transistor, has three

81

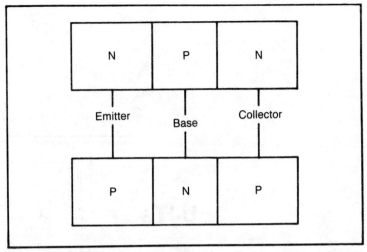

Fig. 4-1. A bipolar transistor can be thought of as a "semiconductor sandwich."

leads. One is called the emitter (the P-type section in an N-type UJT). There are also two base connections (at either end of the larger N-type section in an N-type UJT) called "base 1" and "base 2."

Essentially, the large N-type section acts as a voltage divider resistor pair, with a diode (the single PN junction) connected to the common ends of the two resistances. A simplified equivalent circuit for an N-type UJT is illustrated in Fig. 4-6.

An important specification for the UJT is the intrinsic standoff

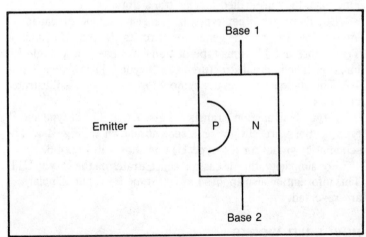

Fig. 4-2. A UJT has just a single PN junction.

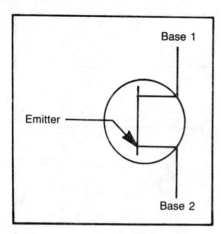

Fig. 4-3. The standard schematic symbol for an N-type UJT.

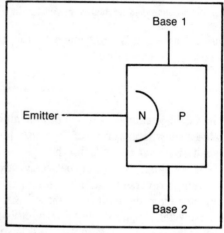

Fig. 4-4. P-type UJTs also exist.

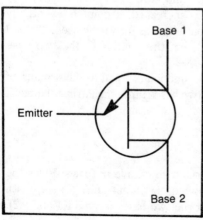

Fig. 4-5. The standard schematic symbol for a P-type UJT.

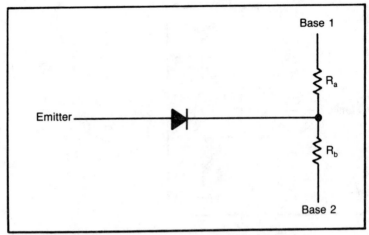

Fig. 4-6. A simplified equivalent circuit for an N-type UJT.

ratio. This value is determined by the internal base resistances, according to this formula:

$$n = Ra/(Ra + Rb)$$

The intrinsic standoff ratio is represented by n. It typically has a value somewhere around 0.5, because the values of Ra and Rb are usually fairly close to each other.

If a voltage is applied between base 1 and base 2, the PN junction is reverse-biased. Naturally, this means that no current can flow from the emitter to either of the base terminals.

Now, let's suppose there is an additional variable voltage source connected between the emitter and base 1, as illustrated in Fig. 4-7. As the emitter voltage is increased, a point is eventually reached where the PN junction becomes forward-biased. Beyond this point, current can flow from the emitter to the two base terminals.

The normal voltage at the junction is equal to the product of the voltage applied across the two bases times the intrinsic standoff ratio. That is:

$$Vj = nV_{BB}$$

When an input pulse with enough amplitude to forward-bias the PN junction in the UJT is applied, an output pulse (in step with the input pulse) will appear at the two bases (across R1 and R2).

These output pulses are usually tapped off across resistor R2. Resistor R1's function is to help keep the circuit operating properly despite any fluctuations in temperature. An additional complimentary (180 degrees out of phase) output may be tapped off across this resistor, which can be useful in certain applications.

The values of these two resistors are usually relatively small. The external resistances are normally considerably smaller than the internal resistances of the UJT itself. This is convenient for analyzing the operation of this device, because we can essentially ignore the external resistances altogether.

The point at which the PN junction becomes forward-biased and begins to conduct can be approximately defined with the following formulas:

$$Vc \ = \ 0.5 \ + \ Vj$$
$$= \ 0.5 \ + \ nVBB$$

Vc is the minimum conduction voltage, Vj is the junction voltage, and VBB is the voltage applied across the two bases. Whenever the input voltage to the emitter exceeds Vc, the UJT conducts.

THE BASIC UJT RELAXATION OSCILLATOR

By adding an RC network to the emitter circuit, as shown in Fig. 4-8, we can build a simple relaxation oscillator. Let's see just how this circuit works.

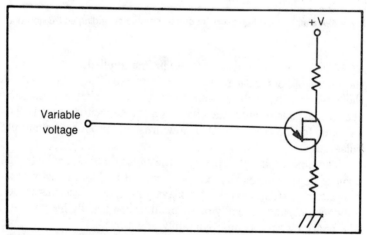

Fig. 4-7. The UJT is usually operated by applying a variable voltage to the emitter.

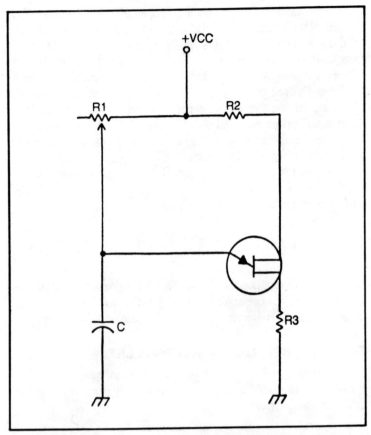

Fig. 4-8. A simple relaxation oscillator can be created by adding an RC network to a UJT.

When the supply voltage (VBB) is first applied to this circuit, the voltage across capacitor C is obviously zero. The voltage across the capacitor immediately starts to increase as the capacitor charges. At some point, the charge on the capacitor exceeds the Vc value for the UJT. The UJT now fires, and produces an output pulse.

The time it takes the charge on the capacitor to reach the firing point is dependent on the values of capacitor C and resistor R3. The intrinsic standoff ratio also plays a part, but since this value is a constant, and normally quite small, it can usually be ignored. The charging time is approximately equal to:

$$T = CR3$$

For example, if C is a 5 μF (0.000005 farad) capacitor, and R3 is a 220 k (220,000 ohm) resistor, the time constant is about:

$$Tc = 0.000005 \times 220000$$
$$= 1.1 \text{ second}$$

When the UJT fires, the capacitor rapidly discharges to ground. This happens very quickly. Once discharged, the cycle repeats, as the capacitor recharges. Since the discharge time is negligible, the output frequency is approximately equal to:

$$F = 1/Tc$$
$$= 1/CR3$$

In our example, using a 5 μF capacitor and a 220 k resistor, the output frequency is about:

$$F = 1/1,1$$
$$= 0.909091 \text{ Hz.}$$

In designing this circuit for a specific desired output frequency it is usually best to select the resistor value, then solve for C:

$$C = 1/FR3$$

The resistance is selected first, because there are more constraints on its value. Ideally, the value of R3 should be between:

$$(V_{BB}(1-n) - 0.5)/2I_p$$

and;

$$(2 \times (V_{BB} - V_v))/I_v$$

Ip is the maximum current flowing from the emitter to base 1. Vv is the valley voltage (the emitter/base 1 voltage just after the UJT has started to conduct), and Iv is the valley current (the emitter/base 1 current when Vv is across the junction). There values can usually be found in the manufacturer's specification sheet.

TYPICAL DESIGN EXAMPLE

Let's work our way through a typical design for this circuit.

The goal is to design a basic UJT relaxation oscillator with an output frequency of 750 Hz, at 2.5 volts peak-to-peak. The output is tapped off across resistor R2.

The UJT used in this design has the following specifications, which are more or less typical:

$$h = 0.52$$
$$Ip = 10 \ \mu A = 0.00001 \ \text{amp}$$
$$Vv = 3.1 \ \text{volt}$$
$$Iv = 25 \ \text{mA} = 0.025 \ \text{amp}$$

Total internal base resistances (Ra + Rb) = 9000 ohms

The first step in designing the circuit is to select the supply voltage (VBB). The sample circuit will operate on 12 volts.

Now you have to find the acceptable range for the value of resistor R3. This resistor should have a value no higher than:

$$
\begin{aligned}
R3I &= (V_{BB}(1-n) - 0.5)/2Ip \\
&= (12(1 - 0.52) - 0.5)/(2 \times 0.00001) \\
&= (12(0.48) - 0.5)/0.00002 \\
&= (5.76 - 0.5)/0.00002 \\
&= 5.71/0.00002 \\
&= 285{,}500 \ \Omega
\end{aligned}
$$

Similarly, the value of R3 should be no lower than:

$$
\begin{aligned}
R3n &= (2(V_{BB} - Vv))/Iv \\
&= (2(12 - 3.1))/0.025 \\
&= (2 \times 8.9)/0.025 \\
&= 17.8/0.025 \\
&= 712 \ \text{ohms}
\end{aligned}
$$

As you can see, you have quite a range of acceptable values for R3. Let's try 22 k (22,000 ohms). This means that for an output frequency of 750 Hz, capacitor C should be equal to:

$$
\begin{aligned}
C &= 1/FR3 \\
&= 1/(750 \times 22000) \\
&= 1/16500000 \\
&= 0.000000061 \ \text{farad} \\
&= 0061 \ \mu F
\end{aligned}
$$

Unfortunately, this is not a standard capacitor value. You might be able to find a 0.062 μF capacitor, but it is quite possible that you will have to settle for a 0.047 μF unit. This changes the output frequency to:

$$
\begin{aligned}
F &= 1/CR3 \\
&= 1/(0.000000047 \times 22000) \\
&= 1/0.001034 \\
&= 967 \text{ Hz.}
\end{aligned}
$$

This isn't very close to the target value of 750 Hz.

Since you have found a capacitance value that almost fits (0.047 μF), you can now go back and calculate a new value for R3 that should still be within the desired range:

$$
\begin{aligned}
R3 &= 1/FC \\
&= 1/(750 \times 0.000000047) \\
&= 1/0.0000353 \\
&= 28.369 \text{ ohms}
\end{aligned}
$$

The nearest standard resistance value is 27 k (27,000 ohms). This is still well within the acceptable range for R3 (712 ohms to 285,500 ohms). Rounding off R3 to 27 k changes the output frequency to:

$$
\begin{aligned}
F &= 1/CR3 \\
&= 1/(0.000000047 \times 27000) \\
&= 1/0.001269 \\
&= 788 \text{ Hz}
\end{aligned}
$$

This should be close enough for most applications. After all, component tolerances might account for this much error. If a more precise frequency is required, try placing a 2.5 k trimpot in series with R3. This allows the actual resistance to vary from 27,000 to 29,500 ohms. Since the nominally ideal value for this resistor is 28,369, you have plenty of elbow room on either side of the desired value to compensate for any reasonable component tolerances.

Now, what about the values of R1 and R2? The equation for the ideal value of R1 is:

$$
R1 = (Ra + Rb)/(2nV_{BB})
$$

This works out to a resistance of:

$$R1 = 9000/(2 \times 0.52 \times 12)$$
$$= 9000/12.48$$
$$= 721 \text{ ohms}$$

R1 almost always has a value in the 500 to 1000 ohm range. Actually, the exact value is not terribly critical. You can easily round the value of R1 off to the nearest standard value available. In this case, you can use either a 750 ohm or a 680 ohm resistor.

Now, you need to find a suitable value for R2. The formula is:

$$R2 = \{V_o[(R_a + R_b) + R1]\}/(V_{BB} - V_o)$$

Vo is the desired peak-to-peak output voltage across R2.

For this example, resistor R2 should have a value of approximately:

$$R2 = (2.5 \times (9000 + 680)/(12 - 2.5)$$
$$= (2.5 \times 9680)/9.5$$
$$= 24200/9.5$$
$$= 2547 \ \Omega$$

Once again, this value is not extremely critical; you can use either a 2.2 k or a 2.7 k resistor.

The signal tapped off across R2 is an ascending sawtooth wave. (See Fig. 4-9.) A descending sawtooth wave can be obtained across R1.

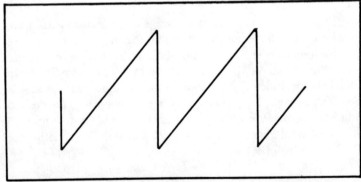

Fig. 4-9. The signal tapped off across R2 will be an ascending sawtooth wave.

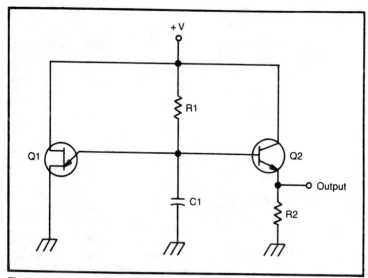

Fig. 4-10. This circuit is an improved sawtooth wave generator.

SAWTOOTH WAVE GENERATORS

As you saw in the simple sample circuit, the UJT is naturally inclined towards generating sawtooth waves. Most practical transistor-based sawtooth wave generators incorporate an UJT.

Sawtooth waves (sometimes called ramp waves) are employed in a wide variety of control applications. For example, a sawtooth wave is used to move the electron beam across the screen of a television set's picture tube.

A slightly improved sawtooth wave generator circuit is illustrated in Fig. 4-10. This circuit operates in a similar manner as the one shown back in Fig. 4-8. Capacitor C1 charges through resistor R1. When the charge on C1 exceeds the UJT's trigger voltage, Q1 fires, producing a narrow pulse which quickly discharges the capacitor. The process then starts over for the next cycle.

The main difference here is the addition of transistor Q2. This transistor amplifies and buffers the charging voltage across the capacitor. An ascending sawtooth wave appears at the output. Resistor R2 is a simple load resistor. Its value should be approximately equal to the input impedance of whatever the generator is driving.

As in the earlier circuit, the output frequency is determined by the R1/C1 time constant.

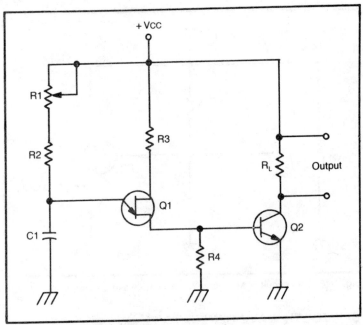

Fig. 4-11. This improved sawtooth wave generator circuit can produce a wide range of output frequencies.

A more practical variation of this circuit is shown in Fig. 4-11. This circuit can put out a very wide range of output frequencies. Potentiometer R1 serves as a manual frequency control. A typical parts list for this circuit is given in Table 4-1. For these component

Table 4-1. Typical Parts List for the Sawtooth Wave Generator Circuit of Fig. 4-11.

Q1	2N2646 UJT
Q2	2N3904 NPN transistor
R1	1 Meg (1,000,000 ohm) potentiometer
R2	3.9K (3900 ohm) resistor
R3	4.7K (4700 ohm) resistor
R4	100 ohm resistor
R_L	selected to match output load
C1	10 μF capacitor
V_{cc}	9 volts

values, the circuit covers the entire audible range of frequencies (approximately 20 Hz to 20 kHz) and even extend somewhat into the subaudible and ultraaudible regions. Because of the wide range, tuning a specific frequency can be a problem. Using a ten-turn potentiometer for R1 makes tuning more convenient.

Another variation on the basic sawtooth wave generator circuit is illustrated in Fig. 4-12. The primary difference here is that the capacitor is charged through a constant current source (Q1), rather than through a simple resistor. This results in a straighter, more linear ramp as the capacitor charges evenly. A constant current source charges a capacitor linearly, while a simple resistor charges a capacitor in an exponential manner.

In this circuit, the charging rate, and therefore the frequency, can be adjusted via potentiometer R2. A smaller resistance here results in a higher output frequency. If you build this circuit using

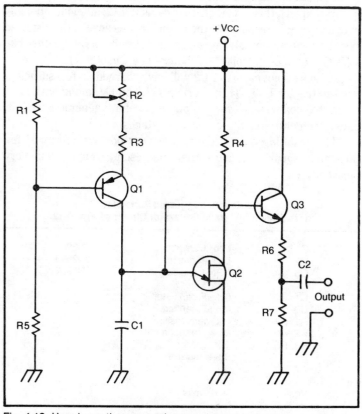

Fig. 4-12. Here is another sawtooth wave generator circuit.

the component values listed in Table 4-2 you will get an output range from slightly less than 100 Hz to well over 1000 Hz.

UNUSUAL WAVEFORM GENERATOR

The last chapter looked at several circuits that generated non-standard waveforms. One more unusual waveform generator circuit is shown in Fig. 4-13. A typical parts list for this circuit is given in Table 4-3.

The output signal from this circuit is extremely unusual. I strongly recommend that you breadboard this circuit, and experiment with various component values while monitoring the waveshape at the output with an oscilloscope.

A fairly standard, albeit distorted sawtooth wave is initially generated by Q1, R1, R2, R3, and C1. This signal drives Q2, which functions as a current source charging C2. Unlike the sawtooth wave generator using a constant current source (presented earlier in this chapter), this circuit charges capacitor C2 at an intentionally irregular rate, in response to the instantaneous level of the distorted sawtooth wave from Q1. In a sense, this circuit operates rather like a VCO (voltage-controlled oscillator—see Chapter 7).

At some point capacitor C2 will have charged up to a sufficient level to trigger UJT Q4 into firing. Q3, and Q4, along with their associated components, form another waveform generation circuit, under the control of the preceeding stages.

The resulting output signal is a very odd waveform. If fed through a speaker, I doubt that the results would sound very pleasant.

**Table 4-2. Suggested Parts List
for the Sawtooth Wave Generator Circuit of Fig. 4-12.**

Q1	PNP transistor	2N3906
Q2	UJT transistor	2N2646
Q3	NPN transistor	2N3904
C1	0.1 μF capacitor	
C2	0.5 μF capacitor	
R1, R4	680 ohm resistor	
R2	25 k potentiometer	
R3, R6	1 k resistor	
R5	3.3 k resistor	
R7	4.7 k resistor	
Vcc	+ 12 volts	

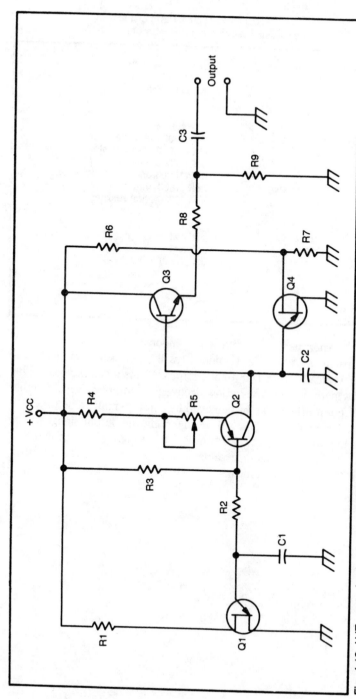

Fig. 4-13. UJTs can also be used to generate nonstandard waveforms.

95

Q1,Q4	2N2646 UJT
Q2	2N3906 PNP
Q3	2N3904 NPN
R1	680 ohm resistor
R2	18K (18000 ohm) resistor
R3	33K (33000 ohm) resistor
R4	12K (12000 ohm) resistor
R5	10K (10000 ohm) potentiometer
R6,R7,R9	1.8K (1800 ohm) resistor
R8	2.2K (2200 ohm) resistor
C1	see text
C2	see text
C3	0.5 μF capacitor
V_{cc}	12 volt

Experiment with different component values, especially for capacitors C1 and C2. Usually C1 will have a relatively large value, typically from 1 μF to 50 μF, or so. This gives the controlling sawtooth wave a very low frequency. Interesting, altogether different effects can be achieved by using a small value for C1. If C2 has a value of about 0.1 μF to 0.5 μF, the output signal will be in the audible range, and can be fed through a loudspeaker.

Different resistance values can also have a significant effect on the output waveform.

Op Amp Circuits

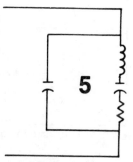 5

THESE DAYS, INTEGRATED CIRCUITS, OR ICS, ARE BEING USED for more and more applications. Without a doubt, the most popular and widespread type of IC is the operational amplifier, or op amp. As it happens, the op amp is very well suited to signal generation applications.

This chapter looks at a few of the many ways an op amp can be used to generate various waveforms, ranging from standard sine waves, triangle waves, and rectangle waves to some very complex and unusual waveforms.

SINE WAVE OSCILLATORS

It was mentioned in earlier chapters that it is difficult to generate a truly pure, distortion-free sine wave. However, it is possible to come very close to an ideal sine wave with an op amp-based oscillator circuit.

A typical op amp sine wave oscillator circuit is shown in Fig. 5-1. The secret to this circuit lies in the feedback network, which is this case is a twin-T network. Similar networks are often used in filter circuits. Resistors R1 and R2, along with capacitor C1, form one T. The other T is made up of R3, R4, C2 and C3. The second T is drawn upside down in the schematic.

The formula for the output frequency from this circuit is:

$$F = 1/(2 \pi R1C2)$$

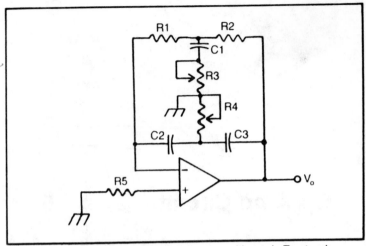

Fig. 5-1. An op amp can generate sine waves with a twin-T network.

where π is pi, a constant with a value of about 3.14.

The formula assumes that the following relationships of component values are true:

$$R2 = R1$$
$$R3 = R1/4$$
$$R4 = R1/2 \text{ (approximate)}$$
$$C1 = 2C2$$
$$C3 = C2$$

If these value relationships are not maintained, the circuit will not function properly, and may not be able to break into oscillations at all.

The twin-T feedback network is detuned slightly by adjusting the value of R4. This component is usually a miniature trimmer potentiometer. The procedure starts by setting the potentiometer to its maximum resistance. Then the resistance is slowly decreased until the circuit just begins to oscillate. If the resistance of R4 is decreased below this point, the sine wave is distorted at the output.

This circuit works because the twin-T network phase shifts the output signal by 180 degrees before feeding it back into the inverting input of the op amp. By definition, the inverting input adds another 180 degrees of phase shift for a total shift of 360 degrees. In other words, you have positive feedback. Internal noise within the IC itself generates enough of a signal to start the oscillation process whenever power is applied to the circuit.

Let's work through a typical design example using this circuit. Your goal is a sine wave oscillator with an output frequency of 600 Hz. The first step in designing the circuit is to select a reasonable value for the capacitor. Try a 0.01 μF capacitor for C2 (and C3—remember, these two capacitors must have identical values).

Now, by algebraically rearranging the basic frequency equation, you can solve for the necessary value of resistor R1:

$$R1 = 1/(2 \pi FC2)$$
$$= 1/(6.28 \times 600 \times 0.00000001)$$
$$= 1/0.0000377$$
$$= 26.526$$

A 27 k resistor should be close enough.

The hard part of the design is done now. It's no problem at all to find the values for the other components in the circuit:

$$R2 = R1$$
$$= 27 \text{ k}$$
$$R3 = R1/4$$
$$= 27.000/4$$
$$= 675 \text{ ohms}$$

(A 680 ohm resistor may be used for R3.)

$$R4 = R1/2$$
$$= 27000/2$$
$$= 13.500 \text{ ohms}$$

(I'd use a 15 k to 25 k trimpot for R4.)

$$C3 = C2$$
$$= 0.01 \ \mu F$$
$$C1 = 2C2$$
$$= 2 \times 0.01 \ \mu F$$
$$= 0.02 \ \mu F$$

And that's all there is to designing this circuit.

Nothing is perfect, and this circuit is no exception to that rule. The major disadvantage of this circuit is that the frequency and purity of the output waveform is dependent on the interrelated

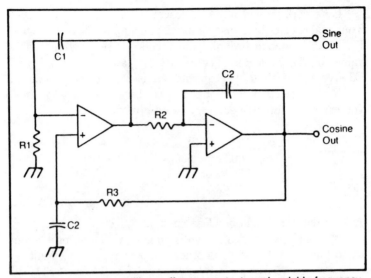

Fig. 5-2. A quadrature oscillator offers two outputs and variable frequency.

values of all of the passive components. There is no easy way to make the output frequency variable.

When a variable output frequency is required, a quadrature oscillator circuit, like the one shown in Fig. 5-2, can be used. A quadrature oscillator has two outputs: labelled "sine" and "cosine." A cosine wave is simply a sine wave that has been phase shifted 90 degrees. This is illustrated in Fig. 5-3.

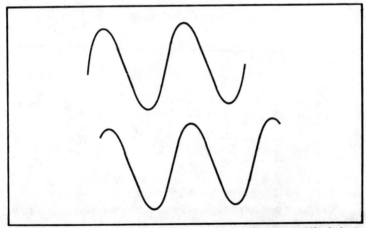

Fig. 5-3. A cosine wave is a sine wave that has been phase shifted ninety degrees.

Probably the first thing you will notice when you look at the circuit in Fig. 5-2 is that two op amps are required for this circuit. Fortunately, op amps ICs are cheap enough these days that this shouldn't be a significant limitation.

Only six passive components are required in addition to the two op amps. This suggests that there won't be very many design calculations. The design process is further simplified by the fact that all three of the capacitors should have identical values. In addition, resistors R2 and R3 are also equal. Resistor R1 is given a value slightly less than that of R2 to make sure that the oscillations begin as soon as power is applied. The exact value is not particularly critical, as long as it is somewhat smaller than R2. The next smaller standard resistance value are normally used for R1.

All of this means that we really only need to determine two component values to design this circuit, C (C1, C2, and C3), and R (R2 and R3).

The frequency equation is the same one used for the twin-T sine wave oscillator discussed above:

$$F = 1/(2 \pi RC)$$

Once again, the best design approach is to arbitrarily select a likely value for C, then rearrange the equation to solve for R:

$$R = 1/(2 \pi FC)$$

As an example, let's design a quadrature oscillator with an output frequency of 1000 Hz. If we use a value of 0.047 μF for C, R should be equal to:

$$\begin{aligned} R &= 1/(6.28 \times 1000 \times 0.000000047) \\ &= 1/0.0002962 \\ &= 3388 \text{ ohms} \end{aligned}$$

As it happens, this is very close to the standard resistor value of 3.3 k. R1 can be the next lower standard resistance value, or 2.7 k. Once again, the exact value of R1 is not particularly critical.

Besides the basic simplicity and elegance of its design, the quadrature oscillator also offers the advantage of a potentially variable output frequency. This can easily be accomplished simply by replacing R2 and R3 with a dual potentiometer. The shafts are ganged together, so these two resistances are always equal, as required by the circuit. Fixed resistors should be used in series with the potentiometers so that the value of R never drops below that of R1.

The sine wave and cosine wave outputs from this circuit always have the same frequency . The only difference between the two output signals is their relative phase.

SQUARE WAVE GENERATORS

An excellent square wave signal can be generated by alternately forcing an op amp into positive and negative saturation. With the right feedback network, this switching can be extremely fast, although not instantaneous. When practical devices are used, a slight slurring is introduced as illustrated in the greatly exaggerated signal shown in Fig. 5-4. This slurring is due to a characteristic of the op amp known as the slew rate. The slew rate determines how fast the output can respond to quick changes in the input signal. The faster the slew rate, the more precise the output waveform.

Most modern op amp ICs have very fast slew rates. Even with an inexpensive "garden variety" op amp like the 741, the slurring is negligible in the vast majority of applications. When a very precise output waveform is required, a high quality op amp IC with a very short slew rate should be used.

Figure 5-5 shows what is probably the simplest possible square wave generator circuit. Besides the op amp itself, only three resistors and a single capacitor are needed to complete the circuit.

Resistor R1 and capacitor C1 are the most important factors in defining the output frequency of this circuit, but the feedback network (R3/R2) also contributes to the output frequency. In oth-

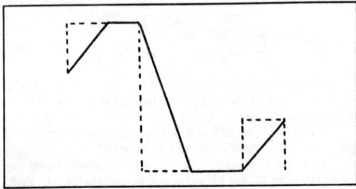

Fig. 5-4. An op amp's slew rate can distort a square wave.

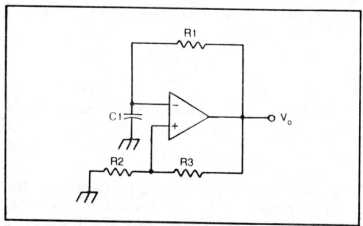

Fig. 5-5. This may be the simplest possible square wave generator circuit.

er words, all of the external passive components in the circuit affect the output frequency.

The exact equations are rather complex, but they can be simplified if you limit yourself to one of two basic R3/R2 ratios. For example, if:

$$R3/R2 = 1{:}1$$

then,

$$F = 0.5/R1C1$$

On the other hand, if:

$$R3/R2 = 10$$
$$F = 5/R1C1$$

Unless there is a very strong reason to do otherwise, it's best to limit yourself to one of these two R3/R2 ratios.

As an example, let's work through the design of a square wave generator. Aim for an output frequency of 1200 Hz, and use an R3/R2 ratio of 10.

The first step in the design is to select an arbitrary value for R2, then find an appropriate value for R3:

$$R3 = R2 \times (R3/R2)$$
$$= R2 \times 10$$

If you use a 22 k resistor R2, then R3 must have a value of:

$$R3 = 22000 \times 10$$
$$= 220000$$
$$= 220 \text{ k}$$

Since the R3/R2 ratio is 10, you know which frequency equation to use:

$$F = 5/R1C1$$

You know you want a value of 1200 Hz. You'll need to find the necessary values for R1 and C1. Simply select a likely value for C1, and then rearrange the equation to solve for R1:

$$R1 = 5/FC1$$

If you select a value of 0.22 μF for C1, then R1's value should be:

$$R1 = 5/(1200 \times 0.00000022)$$
$$= 5/0.000264$$
$$= 18.940 \text{ ohms}$$

A standard 18 k resistor should be close enough for most applications. To determine just how much error has been introduced by rounding off the value of R1, go back to the basic frequency equation:

$$F = 5/R1C1$$
$$= 5/(18000 \times 0.00000022)$$
$$= 5/0.00396$$
$$= 1262.6$$

It's close.

This circuit can be made even more useful by adding a potentiometer, as shown in Fig. 5-6. This allows the output frequency to be manually changed at any time. In this circuit, the value of R1 is equal to the series combination of fixed resistor R1a, and the adjusted value of potentiometer R1b:

$$R1 = R1a + R1b$$

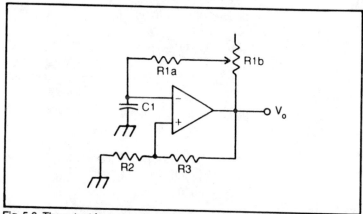

Fig. 5-6. The output frequency from the circuit of Fig. 5-5 can be made variable simply bay adding a potentiometer.

The fixed resistor is included to prevent the value of R1 from becoming zero. The fixed value of R1a determines the maximum output frequency. The series combination when the potentiometer is at its maximum setting determines the minimum output frequency.

To see how this works, assume the circuit includes the following component values:

$$R1a = 10 \text{ k}$$
$$R1b = 50 \text{ k potentiometer}$$
$$R2 = 22 \text{ k}$$
$$R3 = 220 \text{ k}$$
$$C1 = 0.1 \ \mu F$$

Note that feedback resistors R2 and R3 have the same values (and thus the same ratio) as in the previous example. This means we continue to use the same frequency equation.

At the minimum setting of R1b, it's value is essentially 0 ohms, making the total value of R1 equal to R1a

$$R1 = R1a + R1b$$
$$= 10000 + 0$$
$$= 10000 \text{ ohms}$$

At this setting, the output frequency works out to:

$$F = 5/R1C1$$

105

$$= 5/(10000 \times 0.0000001)$$
$$= 5/0.001$$
$$= 5000 \text{ Hz}$$

This is the highest frequency that can appear at the output of this circuit.

Moving potentiometer R1b to its maximum resistance setting changes the combined value of R1 to:

$$R1 = R1a + R1b$$
$$= 10000 + 50000$$
$$= 60000 \text{ ohms}$$

This time, the output frequency works out to:

$$F = 5/R1C1$$
$$= 5/(60000 \times 0.0000001)$$
$$= 5/0.006$$
$$= 633 \text{ Hz}$$

This is the minimum frequency put out by this particular circuit.

For the specified component values in this example, the frequency range is 4167 Hz wide, from 833 Hz to 5000 Hz. Wider or narrower ranges can also be obtained by selecting the correct values for R1a and R1b. If the range is very wide (that is,if the maximum value of R1b is considerably larger than R1a), it is difficult to set the output to a specific desired frequency. A small maximum value for R1b offers a narrower range, but a finer degree of control over the output frequency.

The range can also be altered by changing the value of C1. A switch selectable range features can be added to the circuit by using multiple values for C1 as shown in Fig. 5-7.

As a general rule of thumb, large capacitances and/or large resistances are used for low frequencies. This circuit can remain impressively stable at very low frequencies.

This circuit works by forcing the op amp to switch between positive saturation (maximum positive voltage output) and negative saturation (maximum negative voltage output).

The purest square wave signal can be achieved if R2 has the same value as R3. When the op amp is in positive saturation, the non-inverting input is held at exactly one half of the positive saturation voltage by the feedback loop of R2 and R3. These

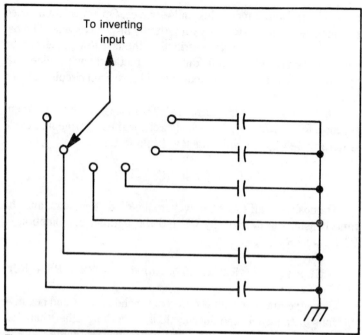

Fig. 5-7. Multiple ranges can be added to the circuits of Fig. 5-5 and 5-6 by switch selecting various values for C1.

resistors act as a simple voltage divider. Almost as good results can be obtained if the R3/R2 ratio is 1:1.

Meanwhile, capacitor C1 is being charged through R1. At some point, the charge on C1 exceeds the voltage at the non-inverting input. Now, the inverting input is more positive than the non-inverting input, forcing the op amp to swing into negative saturation. The non-inverting input is now held at one half the negative saturation voltage by R2 and R3. This condition holds true until capacitor C1 discharges through R1 to less than half the negative saturation voltage. This makes the non-inverting input more positive (less negative) than the inverting input. The op amp switches back into positive saturation, and the cycle repeats.

RECTANGLE WAVE AND PULSE GENERATORS

A square wave is perfectly symmetrical. It is in its high level state for one half of each cycle. In other words, the duty cycle is 1:2. In many applications, rectangle waves with other duty cycles may be needed. Rectangle waves with a very short high level time per cycle are sometimes called pulse waves. Op amps can be used to generate rectangle waves with virtually any duty cycle. The basic square wave generator described in the last few pages can be easily converted into variable duty cycle rectangle wave generator by adding just a few extra components. This revised circuit is shown in Fig. 5-8.

On the negative half-cycles, diode D1 blocks the flow of current through R5 and R6. The time constant for the negative half-cycle is determined by the value of R1, R2, and C1:

$$T2 = C1 \times (R1 + R2)$$

On positive half-cycles, however, the diode conducts, and the time constant is defined by C1 and the parallel combination of R1/R2 and R5/R6:

$$T1 = C1 \times (((R1 + R2) \times (R5 + R6))/(R1 + R2 + R5 + R6))$$

Since the time constant is different for the positive and negative portions of the cycle, the duty cycle is something other than 1:2. The output waveform becomes an asymmetric rectangle wave. A simplified version of this circuit is shown in Fig. 5-9. On positive half-cycles diode D1 is conducting, and diode D2 is blocking the feedbacking path. The positive time constant is simply:

$$T1 = C1 \ R1$$

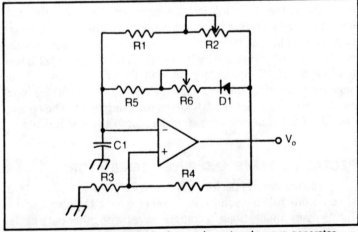

Fig. 5-8. This circuit is a variable duty cycle rectangle wave generator.

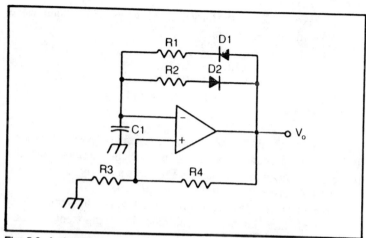

Fig. 5-9. A simplified version of the circuit shown in Fig. 5-8.

On negative half-cycles, the situation is reversed. Diode D1 blocks current flow, while diode D2 conducts through resistor R2. This makes the negative time constant equal to:

$$T2 = C1 \; R2$$

The length of the total cycle is simply the sum of the two half-cycle time constants:

$$Tt = T1 + T2$$

The output frequency is the reciprocal of the total time of the complete cycle:

$$F = 1/Tt$$

The duty cycle, as you should recall, is the ratio between the positive time constant (T1) and the total cycle time (Tt). That is:

$$T1/Tt$$

This can be simplified by factoring:

$$
\begin{aligned}
C1 \; R1 &:(C1 \; R1 + C1 \; R2) \\
&= C1 \; R1/C1:[(C1 \; R1/C1) + (C1 \; R2/C1)] \\
&= R1:(R1 + R2)
\end{aligned}
$$

109

If R1 is equal to R2, the duty cycle becomes 1:2. A square wave is generated by the circuits:

$$R1:(R1 + R1)$$
$$= R1:2R1$$
$$= (R1/R1):(2R1/R1)$$
$$= 1:2$$

Obviously the diodes are serving no useful purpose in this case. If you want a square wave, use one of the circuits from the preceeding section of this chapter. For non-square rectangle waves, R1 and R2 must have different values.

To get a better idea of how this circuit works, let's take a look at a typical example. Assume the following component values:

$$C1 = 0.1 \ \mu F$$
$$R1 = 10 \ k$$
$$R2 = 22 \ k$$

The positive time constant works out to:

$$T1 = C1 \ R1$$
$$= 0.0000001 \times 10000$$
$$= 0.001 \ second$$

The negative time constant is:

$$T2 = C1 \ R2$$
$$= 0.0000001 \times 22000$$
$$= 0.0022 \ second$$

This means that the complete cycle time is:

$$Tt = T1 + T2$$
$$= 0.001 + 0.0022$$
$$= 0.0032 \ second$$

Taking the reciprocal of the total cycle time, find the output frequency:

$$F = 1/Tt$$
$$= 1/0.0032$$
$$= 312.5 \ Hz$$

You can eliminate a number of these steps by rearranging these equations to come up with a single formula for deriving the output frequency directly:

$$
\begin{aligned}
F &= 1/Tt \\
&= 1/(T1 + T2) \\
&= 1/(C1\ R1 + C1\ R2) \\
&= 1/(C1\ (R1 + R2))
\end{aligned}
$$

You can confirm the validity of these new equation by plugging in the same component values we just used with the original equations:

$$
\begin{aligned}
F &= 1/(0.0000001 \times (10000 + 22000)) \\
&= 1/(0.0000001 \times 32000) \\
&= 1/0.0032 \\
&= 312.5\ \text{Hz}
\end{aligned}
$$

Notice that you get exactly the same result with either method. Now, what about the duty cycle? Earlier, we concluded that the duty cycle can be determined directly with just the two resistor values (R1 and R2):

$$
\begin{aligned}
R1&:(R1 + R2) \\
&= 10000:(10000 + 22000) \\
&= 10000:32000 \\
&= (10000/10000):(32000/10000) \\
&= 1:3:2
\end{aligned}
$$

For all intents and purposes, you can round this off to 1:3.

In designing a rectangle wave generator for a specific output signal, first select a reasonable value for capacitor C1. Then rearrange the frequency equation to solve for the combined value (sum) of resistors R1 and R2:

$$
(R1 + R2) = 1/FC1
$$

To separate the values of R1 and R2, you need to decide on the waveform's duty cycle. This ratio will always be in the form of 1:X. The total cycle time, by definition, is equal to the following equation:

$$
Tt = XT1
$$

By the same token, the total resistance is equal to:

$$Rt = XR1$$

This equation can be more conveniently rewritten in the form:

$$R1 = Rt/X$$

Once you know the value of R1, it is a simple enough matter to find the value of R2:

$$R2 = Rt - R1$$

Now, let's try out a typical example by designing a rectangle wave generator with an output frequency of 1400 Hz, and a duty cycle of 1:4. First, select a value for C1. Try a 0.033 μF capacitor. This makes the value of Rt (R1 + R2) equal to:

$$
\begin{aligned}
Rt &= 1/FC1 \\
&= 1/(1400 \times 0.000000033) \\
&= 1/0.0000462 \\
&= 21.645 \text{ ohms}
\end{aligned}
$$

Now you can solve for R1:

$$
\begin{aligned}
R1 &= Rt/X \\
&= 21645/4 \\
&= 5411 \text{ ohms}
\end{aligned}
$$

You can round this off to the standard resistance value, 5.6 k. This gives R2 a value of:

$$
\begin{aligned}
R2 &= Rt - R1 \\
&= 21645 - 5600 \\
&= 16045 \text{ ohms}
\end{aligned}
$$

The nearest standard resistance value is 15 k

Let's see how this rounding off of the resistor values affects the duty cycle:

$$
\begin{aligned}
R1&:(R1 + R2) \\
&= 5600:(5600 + 15000)
\end{aligned}
$$

$$= 5600{:}20600$$
$$= (5600/5600){:}(20600/5600)$$
$$= 1{:}3.68$$

This is close to 1:4. The rounding off error probably won't matter too much in most practical applications. In critical applications, a trimpot can be used in series with one or both of the resistances to permit fine tuning.

Finally, let's double-check the output frequency, since it too is affected by rounding off the resistor values. For our example, the actual output frequency works out to:

$$\begin{aligned} F &= 1/(C1(R1 + R2)) \\ &= 1/(0.000000033 \times (5600 + 15000)) \\ &= 1/(0.000000033 \times 20600) \\ &= 1/0.006798 \\ &= 1471 \text{ Hz} \end{aligned}$$

This is a little high, but still fairly close to our nominal design goal value of 1400 Hz.

TRIANGLE WAVE GENERATORS

Since the harmonic structure of a triangle wave is so similar to that of a square wave, it is not difficult to convert one into the other. As explained in Chapter 1, both of these waveforms are made up of the fundamental and all of the odd harmonics. The difference between the two types of waveforms is that the harmonics are weaker (have a lower amplitude) in the triangle wave, while the harmonics are stronger (have a higher amplitude) in the square wave.

Passing a square wave through a low-pass filter, or an integrator, produces a triangle wave at the output. Most triangle wave generators built around op amps employ this approach. A typical circuit is shown in Fig. 5-10. Op amp A is wired as a comparator. It generates a square wave signal. This signal is passed through op amp B, which is connected as an integrator. This portion of the circuit converts the original square wave into a triangle wave.

The square wave swings back and forth between the op amp's positive and negative saturation voltages. The amplitude of the triangle wave is controlled by the ratio of resistors R2 and R1. These components also affect the output frequency, making adjustment a little tricky. The output frequency is also controlled

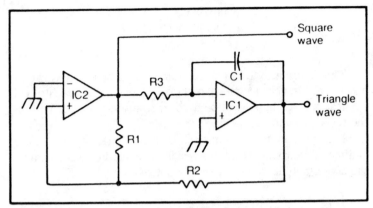

Fig. 5-10. Op amp triangle wave generators are generally in two stages—a square wave generator and a low-pass filter.

by the values of resistor R3 and capacitor C1. In addition to the final triangle wave, it is also possible to tape off the square wave. Of course, both of the output waveforms have the same frequency. The complete formula for the output frequency is:

$$F = (1/(4R3C1)) \times (R1/R2)$$

Actually, since this circuit can simultaneously generate more than one waveform, it is actually a function generator.

SAWTOOTH WAVE GENERATORS

The basic square wave/rectangle wave generators described earlier in this chapter can also be used to generate sawtooth waves. To obtain a sawtooth wave, the output is taken across the capacitor, as illustrated in Fig. 5-11. The capacitor is charged on the positive half-cycle and discharged on the negative half-cycle, producing a modified sawtooth wave across the capacitor, as shown in Fig. 5-12.

The shorter the discharge time (negative half-cycle) in comparison with the charge time (positive half-cycle), the better and more linear the sawtooth shape of the output signal will be. This simple circuit cannot generate a true sawtooth wave, but it can come quite close.

To design this circuit, use the steps for designing a very narrow rectangle wave. Use a duty cycle of 1:10, or better.

An improved op amp sawtooth wave generator circuit is shown

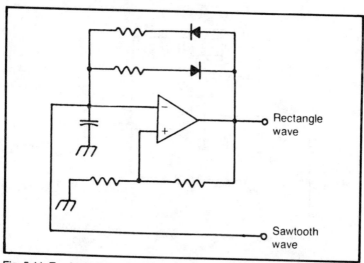

Fig. 5-11. To obtain a modified sawtooth wave, the output is taken off across the capacitor.

in Fig. 5-13. This circuit produces a much more linear output. The feedback resistors and diodes are replaced by transistor Q1. This component is a FET (Field Effect Transistor). Resistor R1 biases the FET to pinch-off.

Capacitor C1 is charged linearly during the positive half-cycle because the FET functions as a constant current source. When the voltage across the capacitor exceeds the positive feedback voltage at the non-inverting input of the op amp, the device switches to negative saturation. The FET in the inverting input feedback path now appears to be a forward-biased diode, allowing capacitor C1

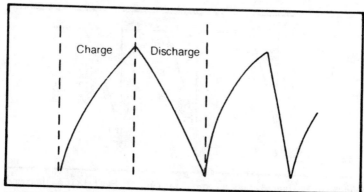

Fig. 5-12. This is the signal that appears across the capacitor in Fig. 5-11.

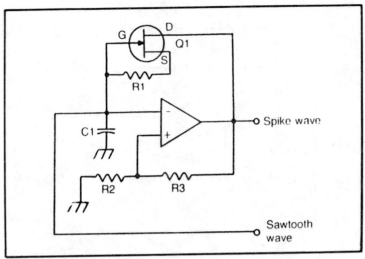

Fig. 5-13. Here is an improved op amp sawtooth generator circuit.

to rapidly discharge. Once C1 is discharged, the op amp switches back to its positive saturation condition and a new cycle begins.

If you tap the output signal from the output of the op amp, you will not get a rectangle wave, but the rather odd negative spike wave illustrated in Fig. 5-14. Each time the op amp switches to negative saturation, a brief negative spike appears at its output. The rest of the time, the op amp's output remains at the positive saturation voltage.

Calculating the output frequency for this circuit is a bit awkward. You must know the op amp's positive saturation voltage (Vs) and the constant pinch-off current of the FET (Ids). These

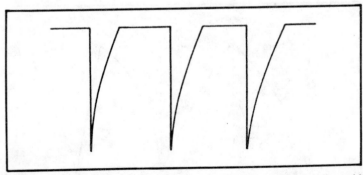

Fig. 5-14. The output of the op amp in the circuit of Fig. 5-13 is a rather odd negative spike wave.

values must be obtained from the specification sheets for the particular devices used. The output frequency formula is:

$$F = Ids/(2 Vs C1 \times (I + (R3/R2)))$$

If you use a circuit with more than one op amp, you can generate an even more linear sawtooth wave. A typical multiple op amp sawtooth wave generator circuit is shown in Fig. 5-15. Unlike the sawtooth wave generators discussed so far in this chapter, this one is not a variation on the basic rectangle wave generator.

For this circuit to function properly, the resistor values must have certain relationships. Specifically, the following conditions must be true:

$$R1 = R2$$
$$R3 = R1/2$$
$$R4 = R5$$
$$R6 = R4/2$$
$$R8 = R9$$

In this circuit, IC1 is a comparator, IC2 is an inverter, and IC3 is a linear integrator. Separate op amp ICs may be used, or these may be different sections of a multiple op amp IC, like the 747 (dual 741 op amp) or the 324 (quad 741 op amp).

The positive feedback loop through R1 around IC1 and IC2 latches these devices until the signal from IC3 (through R2) fires the comparator.

When the output of op amp IC2 is negative, it is fed into the inverting input of op amp IC3 through resistor R8. Diode D3 blocks the current flow through resistor R7. This causes the op amp IC3 to integrate positively at a rate defined as T1. This time constant is defined by the values of capacitor C1 and resistor R8:

$$T1 = C1 R8$$

When the output voltage equals the latching voltage set by zener diodes D1 and D2, the comparator (IC1) reverses its output stage. This makes the output of IC2 positive. Diode D1 now conducts, and the signal is fed into the inverting input of op amp IC3 through the parallel combination of R7 and R8. This discharges capacitor C1 at a rate labelled T2. This time constant is controlled

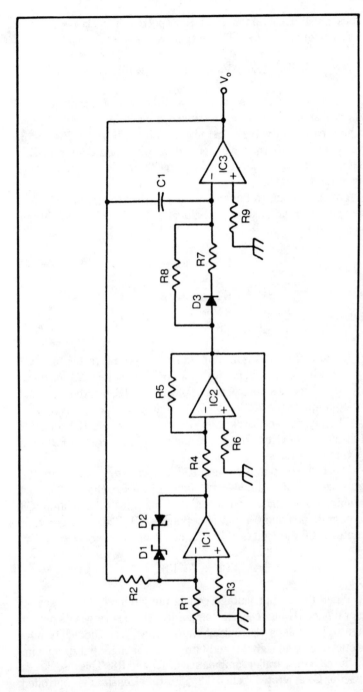

Fig. 5-15. If you use a circuit with more than one op amp, you can generate an even more linear sawtooth wave.

by the values of capacitor C1, and resistors R7 and R8:

$$T2 = C1 \times [(R7 \times R8)/(R7 + R8)]$$

If the value of R7 is made much smaller than that of R8, the discharge rate can be made very steep, improving the linearity of the output waveform.

When the output voltage equals the inverse of the voltage set by the zener diodes (i.e., $V_o = -V_z$), the comparator (IC1) reverts to its original state, and the entire cycle repeats.

Obviously, the complete cycle time equals the sum of the charging time (T1) and the discharging time (T2):

$$\begin{aligned}
Tt &= T1 + T2 \\
&= (C1\ R8) + \{C1 \times [(R7 \times R8)/(R7 + R8)] \} \\
&= C1 \times \{R8 + [(R7 \times R8)/(R7 + R8)] \} \\
&= C1 \times \{ [R8\ (2R7 + R8)]/(R7 + R8) \}
\end{aligned}$$

The output frequency equals the reciprocal of the cycle time:

$$\begin{aligned}
F &= 1/Tt \\
&= 1/C1 \times \{ [R8\ (2R7 + R8)]/(R7 + R8) \}
\end{aligned}$$

A rectangle wave made up of positive pulses can also be tapped off at the output of op amp IC2.

Each of the circuits described in this section generates ascending sawtooth waves. If a descending sawtooth wave is needed, an ascending sawtooth wave can be fed through an inverting voltage follower, as illustrated in Fig. 5-16. Descending sawtooth waves can be generated directly by reversing the polarity at D3 in the circuit of Fig. 5-15. This reverses time constants T1 and T2.

Remember, to create a linear sawtooth wave with this circuit (either the ascending or descending form), resistor R7 must have a much smaller value than resistor R8. If R7 is much larger than R8, a signal that is similar to a triangle wave will be generated. A number of very unusual waveforms can be created by experimenting with the relative values of R7 and R8. Bear in mind that changing either or both of these resistances has an effect on the output frequency.

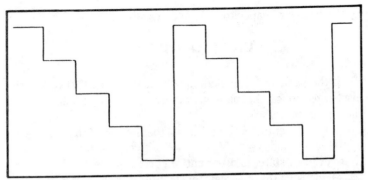

Fig. 5-16. A descending sawtooth wave can be obtained by passing an ascending sawtooth wave through an inverting voltage follower.

STAIRCASE WAVE GENERATORS

A rather novel waveform that can easily be generated by an op amp circuit is the staircase wave. There are numerous variations with different numbers of steps. A typical staircase wave is shown in Fig. 5-17. Some staircase waves descend rather than ascend. Others alternate ascending and descending patterns, as illustrated in Fig. 5-18.

The circuit illustrated in Fig. 5-19 can derive a descending staircase wave from a square wave. Assuming capacitor C2 is fully discharged, the initial output is at the positive saturation voltage. For each positive pulse received at the input, the output voltage drops a step.

The amplitude drop of each step can be found with the following equation:

$$V_s = - \{ [C1 \times (V1 - 2Vd)]/C2 \}$$

Vs is the step voltage, V1 is the peak-to-peak voltage of the input pulse(s), and Vd is the voltage drop across each of the diodes. These diodes should be very closely matched so that Vd1 = Vd2. At some point the op amp reaches its negative saturation point. Of course, there can be no further steps down in the output voltage after that.

The output level can be reset back to the original positive saturation voltage by momentarily closing switch S1, allowing capacitor C2 to completely discharge. In practical circuits, this switch is replaced by an electronic switch that automatically performs the switching operation at a rate equal to the frequency of the output signal.

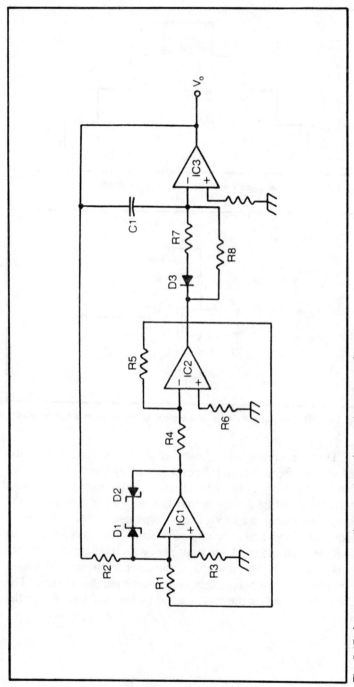

Fig. 5-17. An op amp can easily generate various staircase waveforms.

121

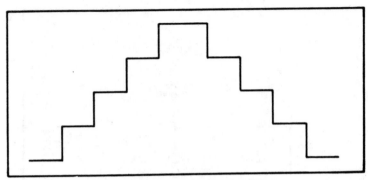

Fig. 5-18. Some staircase waves go both up and down.

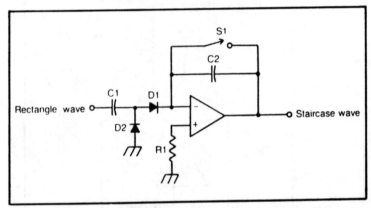

Fig. 5-19. This circuit creates a descending staircase from a square wave.

The number of steps in the staircase wave depends on the ratio of the input frequency to the reset frequency (output frequency). The input frequency must be higher than the output frequency.

If the input frequency is four times the reset frequency, the output waveform consists of four steps per cycle. If the input frequency is five times the reset frequency, the staircase wave at the output is made up of five steps per cycle. If the input frequency is not an exact integer multiple of the reset frequency, the output waveform may not always contain the same number of steps. The first and last steps in the cycle may be shorter in duration than the middle steps.

Timer Circuits 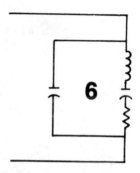 6

THE OP AMP, DISCUSSED IN THE LAST CHAPTER, IS PROBABLY the most popular type of analog IC. The second most popular type is the timer. Timer ICs are used primarily in multivibrator circuits. A multivibrator is a circuit that switches between two output states (HIGH and LOW). There are three types of multivibrators:

☐ The monostable multivibrator has one stable state. When a trigger pulse is received by the circuit, the output goes to the opposite (unstable) state for a predetermined length of time.

☐ The bistable multivibrator has two stable states. Each time a trigger pulse is received by the circuit, the output reverses states. Either output condition can be held indefinitely.

☐ The astable multivibrator has no stable states. It automatically and continuously switches back and forth between states at a predetermined rate.

Timer ICs are normally used in monostable and astable multivibrator circuits. The astable multivibrator is essentially a rectangle wave generator, so it is of interest to us in this book.

THE BASIC 555 ASTABLE MULTIVIBRATOR CIRCUIT

Without any question, the most popular timer IC is the 555. This eight pin device is shown in Fig. 6-1. This chip has a lot going

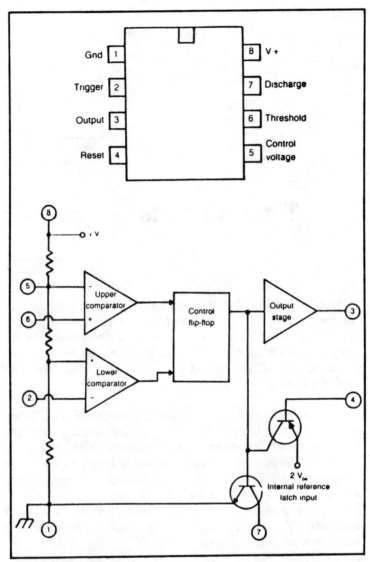

Fig. 6-1. The 555 is a very popular timer IC.

for it. It is widely available, and very inexpensive (usually well under a dollar—often less than fifty cents). It is very easy to use; only a handful of external components are required for most practical applications.

Another significant factor in the 555's immense popularity is the fact that the inherent limitations of an inexpensive timer can be virtually ignored in the vast majority of practical applications. An inexpensive op amp IC, like the 741 for example, produces a noticeable amount of noise, and may have an excessive slew rate for all but the most non-critical applications. The chief shortcoming of an inexpensive timer IC like the 555 is that there is some imprecision in the timing interval. But if standard resistors and capacitors are used in the circuit, they introduce far more timing error than the IC. If the circuit is critical at all, a variable component (usually a potentiometer) must be used to fine tune the timing interval, correcting for any component tolerances, including any imprecision from the IC. In other words, the 555's imprecision is completely irrelevant in the vast majority of applications.

The basic 555 astable multivibrator circuit is illustrated in Fig. 6-2. Notice how simple this circuit is. Only four external components are required: two resistors, and two capacitors. As a matter of fact, capacitor C2 is actually optional. It is included to improve the stability of the circuit. In many cases, it wouldn't be missed at all if omitted. However, I think it is a good idea to always include C2, just in case. It's cheap insurance. This component should have a capacitance between about 0.001 μF and 0.01 μF. The exact value doesn't matter. If you use a cheap ceramic disc capacitor (and there is no point in using anything better), including C2 only adds a dime

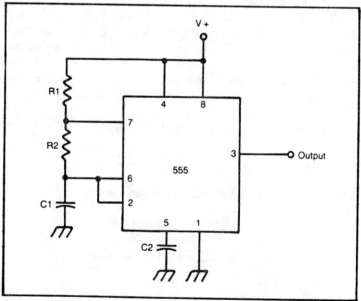

Fig. 6-2. Basic 555 astable multivibrator (rectangle wave generator) circuit.

or so to the circuit cost. The other three external components (R1, R2, and C1) help determine the output frequency and duty cycle.

Notice also that the trigger input (pin #2) is shorted to the threshold input (pin #6). This connection is what forces the timer to operate in its astable mode.

When power is initially applied to this circuit, the voltage across timing capacitor C1 is low, of course. As a result of this low voltage, the timer is triggered (through pin #2). The output goes to its high state, and the IC's internal discharge transistor (at pin #7) is turned off. A complete current path through C1, R1, and R2 is formed, charging the capacitor.

When the charge on C1 exceeds two-thirds of the supply voltage, the timer's upper threshold is reached. This voltage on pin #6 forces the output back to its LOW state.

Timing capacitor C1 now starts to discharge through resistor R2, but not R1 because the internal transistor (at pin #7) is now turned on. When the voltage across C1 drops below one third of the supply voltage, the timer is automatically retriggered, and a new cycle begins.

The exact supply voltage isn't really critical. The timing is derived by the IC's internally determined ratios. The supply voltage does not affect the timing cycles. The 555 timer can be reliably powered by anything from +4.5 volts to +15 volts.

Typical timing signals within this circuit are illustrated in Fig. 6-3. Since both resistors (R1 and R2) affect the charging time (high output, or T1), and only R2 affects the discharging time (low output, or T2), the low output time must always be at least slightly less than the high output time. A true 50 percent duty cycle square wave is not possible with this circuit, although you can come close if the value of R1 is relatively small.

The charging time (high output time) equals:

$$T1 = 0.693(R1 + R2)C1$$

while the discharging time (LOW output time) equals:

$$T2 = 0.693R2C1$$

The total cycle time is simply the sum of the charging and discharging times):

$$Tt = T1 + T2$$

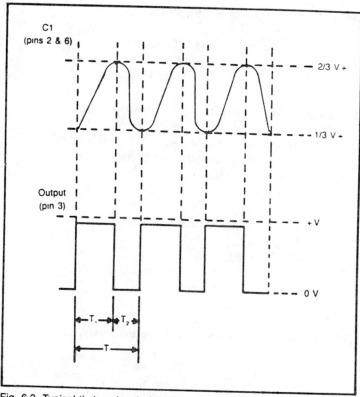

Fig. 6-3. Typical timing signals for the circuit of Fig. 6-2.

$$= 0.693(R1 + R2)C1 + 0.693R2C1$$
$$= 0.693(R1 + 2R2)C1$$

The frequency of the output signal is the reciprocal of the total cycle time. That is:

$$F = 1/T$$
$$= 1/[0.693(R1 + R2)C1]$$
$$= 1.44/[R1 + R2)C1]$$

For proper operation, the component values should be held between specific limits. The combined series value (sum) of resistors R1 and R2 should be no less than 10 k and no more than 14 Meg. The timing capacitor (C1) should have a value between about 100 pF and approximately 1000 μF.

Let's work our way through a few simple examples. To begin

with, assume the following component values:

$$R1 = 47 \text{ k } (47,000 \text{ ohms})$$
$$R2 = 47 \text{ k } (47,000 \text{ ohms})$$
$$C1 = 0.1 \text{ } \mu\text{F } (0.0000001 \text{ farad})$$

The output is in its high state for a time equal to:

$$T1 = 0.693 \times (47000 + 47000) \times 0.0000001$$
$$= 0.693 \times 94000 \times 0.0000001$$
$$= 0.0065 \text{ second}$$
$$= 6.5 \text{ mS}$$

The low output time is equal to:

$$T2 = 0.693 \text{ R2C1}$$
$$= 0.693 \times 47000 \times 0.0000001$$
$$= 0.0033 \text{ second}$$
$$= 3.3 \text{ mS}$$

This means a complete cycle lasts approximately:

$$Tt = T1 + T2$$
$$= 6.5 + 3.3$$
$$= 8.8 \text{ mS}$$

Taking the reciprocal of this, you get an approximate output frequency of:

$$F = 1/T$$
$$= 1/0.0098$$
$$= 102 \text{ Hz}$$

You can doublecheck your work by using the alternate form of the frequency equation:

$$F = 1.44/[R1 + 2R2)C1]$$
$$= 1.44/[47000 + (2 \times 47000)] \times 0.0000001$$
$$= 1.44/[(47000 + 94000) \times 0.0000001]$$
$$= 1.44/(141000 \times 0.0000001)$$
$$= 1.44/0.0141$$
$$= 102 \text{ Hz}$$

Now what about the duty cycle? This is the ratio of the high time to the total cycle time, or in terms of our resistance values:

$$(R1 + R2) : (R1 + 2R2)$$
$$(47000 + 47000) : [47000 + (2 \times 47000)]$$
$$94000 : (470000 + 94000)$$
$$94000 : 141000$$
$$1:1.5$$

Notice that using identical values for R1 and R2 certainly does not give us a 1:2 duty cycle.

Let's try a second example. This time, assume the following component values:

$$R1 = 22 \text{ k} \qquad (22,000 \text{ ohms})$$
$$R2 = 820 \text{ k} \qquad (820,000 \text{ ohms})$$
$$C1 = 0.47 \ \mu F \qquad (0.00000047 \text{ farad})$$

The cycle times in this case works out to:

$$T1 = 0.693(22000 + 820000)0.00000047$$
$$= 0.693 \times 842000 \times 0.00000047$$
$$= 0.2742 \text{ second}$$
$$= 274.2 \text{ mS}$$

$$T2 = 0.693R2C1$$
$$= 0.693 \times 820000 \times 0.00000047$$
$$= 0.2671 \text{ second}$$
$$= 267.1 \text{ mS}$$

$$Tt = T1 + T2$$
$$= 0.5413 \text{ second}$$
$$= 541.3 \text{ mS}$$

Note that since R2 is so much larger than R1, the result is much closer to a square wave (1:2 duty cycle):

$$(R1 + R2) : (R1 + 2R2)$$
$$= (22000 + 820000) : [22000 + (2 \times 820000)]$$
$$= 842000 : (22000 + 1640000)$$
$$= 842000 : 1662000$$
$$= 1:197$$

Finally, solve for the output frequency:

$$F = 1.44 / \{[22000 + (2 \times 820000)] \times 0.00000047\}$$

$$= 1.44[(22000 + 1640000) \times 0.00000047]$$
$$= 1.44/(1662000 \times 0.00000047)$$
$$= 1.44/0.78114$$
$$= 1.84 \text{ Hz}$$

In many applications, you will only be interested in the output frequency, and you won't have to bother calculating the timing periods at all.

Large component values result in low output frequencies. For example:

$R1 = 3.3 \text{ Meg}$ (3,300.000 ohms)
$R2 = 10 \text{ Meg}$ (10,000,000 ohms)
$C1 = 1000 \Omega\text{F}$ (0.001 farad)
$F = 1.44/\{[3300000 + (2 \times 10000000)] \times 0.001\}$
$ = 1.44/[(3300000 + 20000000) \times 0.001]$
$ = 1.44/(23300000 \times 0.001)$
$ = 1.44/23300$
$ = 0.000063 \text{ Hz}$
$ = 0.062 \text{ MHz}$

This is one complete cycle about every four and a half hours. This is close to the lower limit for the basic 555 astable multivibrator circuit.

On the other hand, small component values result in high output frequencies. For example, if you choose components close to the minimum acceptable values for this circuit:

$R1 = 6.8 \text{ k}$ (6800 ohms)
$R2 = 3.9 \text{ k}$ (3900 ohms)
$C1 = 100 \text{ pF}$ (0.0000000001 farad)

then the output frequency works out to:

$F = 1.44/[(6800 + (2 \times 3900)] \times 0.0000000001$
$ = 1.44/[(6800 + 7800) \times 0.0000000001]$
$ = 1.44/(14600 \times 0.0000000001)$
$ = 1.44/0.0000146$
$ = 986.301 \text{ Hz}$
$ = 986 \text{ kHz}$

As you can see, this circuit is capable of a very wide range of output frequencies. For stable operation, however, it is not recommended that this circuit be used at frequencies above about 100 kHz, or so. This is due to internal storage times within the 555 chip itself.

Duty cycles of near 50 percent to about 99 percent can be set up with the proper selection of values for R1 and R2. R1 can be as small as 100 ohms, or R2/100, whichever is larger.

Variations On The Basic
555 Astable Multivibrator Circuit

The basic circuit of Fig. 6-2 is very versatile, and a number of interesting variations are possible. The 555 is designed for a rectangle wave output, but other waveforms may be tapped off across the capacitor. (Refer to Fig. 6-3.) The signal across C1 is some form of ramp-like wave. If the duty cycle is close to 50 percent; this signal is a slightly distorted triangle wave. At the other end of the spectrum, a duty cycle above 90 percent converts this signal into a marginally distorted ascending sawtooth wave.

Of course, these waveforms are not very linear. There can also be a problem with loading; it is probably necessary to use a buffer amplifier for almost any practical application.

It is possible to get a more linear sawtooth wave from a 555 timer. A circuit for this is shown in Fig. 6-4. Transistor Q1 is a constant current source. The timing period for the charging cycle is:

$$T1 = ((V_{CC}/3)C1)/It$$

where V_{CC} is the supply voltage, C1 is the capacitance of the timing capacitor, and It is the Q1 current, set up by emitter resistor R3.

For a 15 volt power supply, It is approximately:

$$It = 4.4 \ V/Rt$$

You can combine these two equations to come up with a simpler formula for the charging period:

$$T1 = 1.1R3C1$$

Remember, this equation is only valid when the supply voltage is 15 volts.

The discharge time is made much shorter than the charging

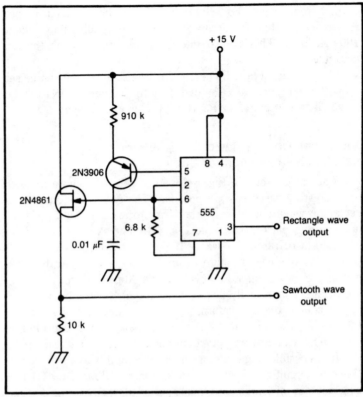

Fig. 6-4. The 555 timer can be forced to generate fairly linear sawtooth waves.

time. The formula is:

$$T2 = 0.7R1C1$$

The discharge period is normally made so short with reference to the charging time, that it can often be effectively ignored. The total cycle time can be considered approximately equal to the charging time:

$$Tt = T1$$
$$= 1.1R3C1$$

As usual, the output frequency is simply the reciprocal of the cycle time period:

$$F = 1/Tt$$

With a little bit of algebraic rearranging, you can solve output frequency directly:

$$F = 0.91/R3\ C1$$

Remember, this equation is an approximation, ignoring the eff of the brief discharge period (T2).

The circuit functions at voltages less than 15 volts, but t equations become increasingly inaccurate as the supply voltage decreased. The FET is included as a buffer amplifier for the ram signal. Notice that the normal pulse output is simultaneously available at pin #3 of the 555. Typical values are shown in the diagram. With the component values listed here, the output frequency will be about 100 Hz.

In the basic 555 astable multivibrator circuit, the charging and discharging periods interact. The addition of a simple diode, as

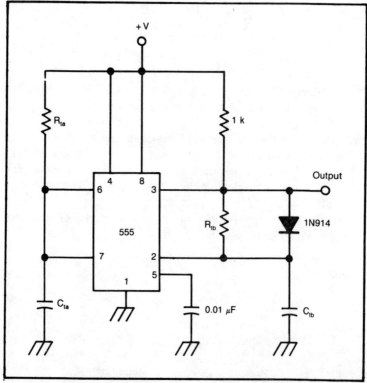

Fig. 6-5. Adding a diode to the basic rectangle wave generator permits independently adjustable timing periods.

133

illustrated in Fig. 6-5 permits independently adjustable timing periods.

The same basic equation is used for both timing periods:

$$t = 0.76 R_t C_1$$

For the charging period (T1), Rt is resistor R1. For the discharging period (T2), resistor R2 is Rt.

The complete timing cycle is just the sum of the charging and discharging periods, of course:

$$\begin{aligned} T_t &= T1 + T2 \\ &= 0.76 R_1 C_1 + 0.76 R_2 C_1 \\ &= 0.76 (R_1 + R_2) C_1 \end{aligned}$$

The output frequency equals:

$$\begin{aligned} F &= 1/T_t \\ &= 1/(0.76(R_1 + R_2)C_1) \\ &= 1.32/((R_1 + R_2)C_1) \end{aligned}$$

Remember that these equations are approximations that are most accurate when the supply voltage is +15 volts.

Because of the diodes in the circuit, the timing periods vary with the supply voltage. The equations given here are most accurate for a supply voltage of +15 volts. Since semiconductors, such as diodes, tend to be temperature sensitive, the timing periods may also fluctuate with the ambient temperature. This effect is minimized with a 15 volt supply voltage.

Let's see how the equations work in a practical example. Use the following component values:

$$\begin{aligned} R_1 &= 22\ k \\ R_2 &= 180\ k \\ C_1 &= 3.3\ \mu F \end{aligned}$$

The charging time equals:

$$\begin{aligned} T1 &= 0.76 \times 22000 \times 0.0000033 \\ &= 0.055\ \text{second} \\ &= 55\ \text{mS} \end{aligned}$$

The discharging time is about:

$$T1 = 0.76 \times 180000 \times 0.0000033$$
$$= 0.451 \text{ second}$$
$$= 451 \text{ mS}$$

So, the total cycle time works out to approximately:

$$Tt = 55 + 451$$
$$= 506 \text{ mS}$$

The duty cycle is:

$$T1 : Tt$$
$$55 : 506$$
$$1:9.2$$

The output frequency can be found either by taking the reciprocal of the total cycle time:

$$F = 1/Tt$$
$$= 1/0.506$$
$$= 1.976 \text{ Hz}$$

or directly from the component values:

$$F = 1.32/[(22000 + 180000) \times 0.00000033]$$
$$= 1.32/(202000 \times 0.0000033)$$
$$= 1.32/0.6666$$
$$= 1.980 \text{ Hz}$$

The small difference between the two results is due to rounding off of values in the timing equations.

Let's try another example:

$$R1 = 820 \text{ k}$$
$$R2 = 100 \text{ k}$$
$$C1 = 0.05 \ \mu F$$
$$T1 = 0.76 \times 820000 \times 0.00000005$$
$$= 0.03116 \text{ second}$$
$$= 31.16 \text{ mS}$$

$$T2 = 0.76 \times 100000 \times 0.00000005$$
$$= 0.0038 \text{ second}$$
$$= 3.8 \text{ mS}$$
$$Tt = 31.16 + 3.8$$
$$= 34.96 \text{ mS}$$

The duty cycle is:

$$31.16 : 34.96$$
$$= 1 : 1.12$$

Finally, the output frequency in this example is approximately:

$$= 1.32/[(820000 + 100000) \times 0.00000005]$$
$$= 1.32/(920000 \times 0.00000005)$$
$$= 1.32/0.046$$
$$= 28.7 \text{ Hz}$$

Many other variations on the basic 555 astable multivibrator circuit are also possible.

MULTIPLE TIMER ICs

In many circuits, more than a single 555 timer may be required. Multiple timers in a single IC package make such systems simpler and more compact.

Figure 6-6 shows the pinout diagram for the 556 IC. This chip is a dual timer device. It contains two separate 555-type timers in a single package. These two timers may be employed together or independently (except for the power supply connections).

The 5558 is a quad timer IC. As the pinout diagram of Fig. 6-7 indicates, this chip contains four 555-type timers. Notice that the pin connections for each timer is somewhat simplified. Some functions that are brought out to pins in the 555 and 556 ICs are internally connected in the 5558. This compromise was made to keep the number of pins on the IC down to a standard 16 DIP size.

THE 2240 PROGRAMMABLE TIMER

The 555 is unquestionably the most popular timer IC around today, but it is not the only one. There are precision timers, such as the 322 and the 3905. Unfortunately for our purposes, these devices are suitable only for monostable operation.

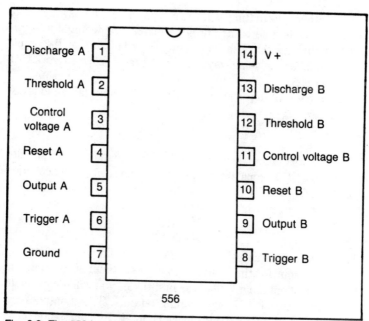

Fig. 6-6. The 556 is a pair of 555 timers in a single IC package.

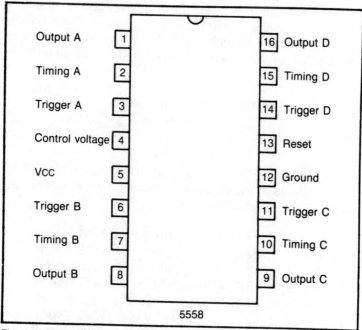

Fig. 6-7. The 5558 is a quad 555 times IC.

137

Another fascinating and versatile timer IC is the 2240 programmable timer. The "programmable" name might lead you to think that this chip is far more complicated to use than the simple 555. But in fact, in some ways the 2240 is even easier to work with than the 555.

The basic timing equation for the 555 (monostable mode) is:

$$T = 1.1RC$$

This isn't very complex, of course. But the equation is even simpler for the 2240. The constant is eliminated. The basic timing equation for the 2240 is:

$$T = RC$$

This is as simple as any timing equation could possibly get.

The pinout for the 2240 programmable timer IC is shown in Fig. 6-8. Undoubtably, one of the first things you will notice about this chip is that it has eight timing outputs. These outputs are actually part of an eight bit binary counter. By combining these outputs in the proper combinations, you can easily create timing periods ranging from 1 to 255 times the basic timing period (T).

The basic timing period (T) is available at pin #1. The remaining outputs are binary multiples of T. To see how this works, let's assume that R is 39 k and C is 0.5 μF. The basic timing period in this example is:

$$
\begin{aligned}
T &= 39000 \times 0.0000005 \\
&= 0.0195 \text{ second} \\
&= 19.5 \text{ mS}
\end{aligned}
$$

When the timer is triggered (at pin #11), a pulse lasting 0.0195 second appears at pin #1. Each of the other output pins will pin out pulses of the following lengths:

Pin #2	2T	= 2 × 0.0195	= 0.039 second
Pin #3	4T	= 4 × 0.0195	= 0.078 second
Pin #4	8T	= 8 × 0.0195	= 0.156 second
Pin #5	16T	= 16 × 0.0195	= 0.312 second
Pin #6	32T	= 32 × 0.0195	= 0.624 second
Pin #7	64T	= 64 × 0.0195	= 1.248 second
Pin #8	128T	= 128 × 0.0195	= 2.496 second

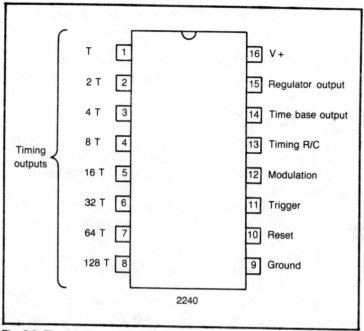

Fig. 6-8. The 2240 programmable timer is a remarkably powerful IC.

All with a single circuit:

And that's not all. You can also combine output pins to create different (non-binary) multiples of the basic timing cycle. For example, if you AND together pins #1, 2, 4, and 7, the output pulse length is:

$$T + 2T + 8T + 64T = 75T$$
$$= 75 \times 0.0195$$
$$= 1.4625 \text{ second}$$

The maximum output pulse is achieved by combining all eight of the outputs:

$$T + 2T + 4T + 8T + 16T + 32T + 64T + 128T = 255T$$
$$= 255 \times 0.0195$$
$$= 4.9725$$

You can select output pulses ranging from just under 20 mS to almost 5 seconds with a single set of component values:

Let's take a quick look at the remaining eight pins on the 2240 IC.

☐ Pin #9, GROUND: the common connection point.

☐ Pin #10, RESET: similar in function to the RESET pin on the 555.

☐ Pin #11, TRIGGER: the input used to trigger the timing cycle.

☐ Pin #12, MODULATION: allows the designer access to the comparator reference voltage (normally 0.731 Vcc). This pin permits simple voltage control of the timing period. (Voltage control is discussed in Chapter 7.)

☐ Pin #13, TIMING R/C: the common connection point for the timing resistor and capacitor, which determine the length of the basic timing period.

☐ Pin #14, TIME BASE OUTPUT: the output of the internal time base oscillator. This pin is normally held HIGH, but it goes low during the timing period cycle.

☐ Pin #15, REGULATOR OUTPUT: the output of an internal voltage regulator stage. If the supply voltage (Vcc) is 5 volts, the regulator voltage is about 4.4 volts. For a supply voltage of 15 volts, the regulator puts out 6.3 volts. If the supply voltage is 4.5 volts or less, this pin should be shorted to Vcc (pin #16).

☐ Pin #16, V+ (or Vcc): the pin for applying the positive supply voltage to the 2240. This chip can be operated on a wide range of supply voltages running from +4 volts to +15 volts.

Like the 555 timer, the 2240 programmable timer can be operated in either a monostable or an astable mode. This book is concerned only with the astable mode.

The basic 2240 astable multivibrator circuit is illustrated in Fig. 6-9. Notice that the outputs are connected with dotted lines. Only the desired outputs should be connected to R1. For a manually programmable selection of outputs, switches can be used to make or break the desired output connections.

The output frequency is determined by the value of R2 and C1, and the selected output pin values. The formula for the output frequency from this circuit is:

$$F = 1/(2NR2\ C1)$$

where N is the count value selected at the output pins. For example,

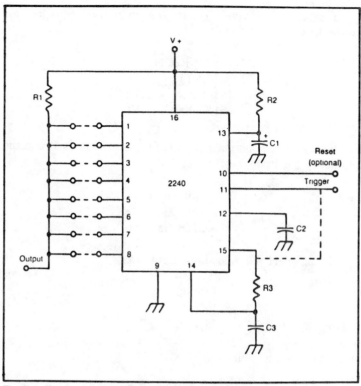

Fig. 6-9. The basic 2240 astable multivibrator circuit.

if output pins #3 (4T) and #5 (16T) are used, then N is equal to:

$$N = 4 + 16$$
$$= 20$$

It is not at all difficult to work with this equation. Let's try out a few examples. First, let's assume the following component values:

$$R2 = 4.7 \text{ k}$$
$$C1 = 0.05 \ \mu\text{F}$$

The basic timing period (T) equals:

$$T = R2 \ C1$$
$$= 4700 \times 0.00000005$$
$$= 0.000235$$

You can substitute T into the frequency equation for convenience:

$$F = 1/(2NR2C1)$$
$$= 1/2NT)$$
$$= 1/(2 \times N \times 0.000235)$$
$$= 1/(0.00047 \times N)$$

If you just use output pin #1 (1T), then N equals 1, and the frequency has its highest value:

$$F = 1/(0.00047 \times 1)$$
$$= 1/0.00047$$
$$= 2128 \text{ Hz}$$

If you select the following output pins:

$$
\begin{array}{ll}
\text{PIN \#2} & \text{4T} \\
\text{PIN \#5} & \text{16T} \\
\text{PIN \#6} & \text{32T}
\end{array}
$$

the N takes on a value of:

$$N = 4 + 16 + 32$$
$$= 52$$

so the frequency becomes equal to:

$$F = 1/(0.00047 \times 52)$$
$$= 1/0.02444$$
$$= 41 \text{ Hz}$$

For proper operation, resistor R2 should have a value between 1 k and 10 Meg, and capacitor C1 should have a value between 0.01 μF and 1000 μF.

Using the minimum component values, and output pin #1, you get the highest possible frequency from this circuit:

$$T = 1000 \times 0.00000001$$
$$= 0.00001$$
$$= 0.01 \text{ mS}$$

$$
\begin{aligned}
F &= 1/(2 \times N \times 0.00001) \\
&= 1/(2 \times 1 \times 0.00001) \\
&= 1/0.00002 \\
&= 50.000 \text{ Hz} \\
&= 50 \text{ kHz}
\end{aligned}
$$

Similarly, by using the largest acceptable component values, and all eight outputs (N = 255), you get the lowest possible frequency:

$$
\begin{aligned}
T &= 10000000 \times 0.001 \\
&= 10000 \text{ seconds} \\
&= 2 \text{ hours, 46 minutes, 40 seconds} \\
F &= 1/(2 \times 255 \times 10000) \\
&= 1/5100000 \\
&= 0.0000001 \text{ Hz}
\end{aligned}
$$

This chip unquestionably has a wide range. From one pulse every 10 μS to one pulse every 708 hours, 20 minutes—that's nearly one pulse a month!

The other components in the circuit are pretty basic. Resistor R1 is a load resistor. The output signal is taken off across this resistor, which usually has a value of about 10 k. Resistor R3 serves as a load resistance for the time base output. A typical value for this resistor is about 22 k.

Capacitor C3 is for added stability. It usually has a value about 0.01 μF. It is only absolutely needed if the timing capacitor (C1) has a value of 0.1 μF or less, and the supply voltage is 7 volts or more, but it is a good idea to always include the stability capacitor as cheap insurance.

This is a triggered astable multivibrator circuit. It does not self-start when power is applied, because the internal logic within the 2240 IC reverts to the reset state. To get the oscillations started, a pulse must be applied to the trigger input (pin #11). The output pulses then continue indefinitely until power is removed from the circuit, or until a pulse is applied to the reset pin (pin #10). This ability to turn the pulses on and off with an electrical signal can be very handy in certain applications, especially those involving automation.

On the other hand, if this triggering feature is not desired, the circuit can be forced to self-start when power is applied simply by shorting the trigger input (pin #11) to the regulator output (pin #15). This connection is shown as a dotted line in the schematic.

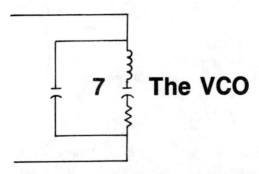

7 The VCO

SO FAR, ALL OF THE OSCILLATOR CIRCUITS DISCUSSED IN CHAP-
ters 2 through 6 either put out a single fixed frequency or a
single manually adjustable frequency. In some applications,
automated control of the output frequency may be desirable, or even
essential. These applications call for the VCO, or voltage-controlled
oscillator.

A VCO, as the name suggests, is simply an oscillator circuit
that puts out a frequency that is proportional to an input voltage.
Some VCOs are actually controlled by an input current, rather than
an input. Strictly speaking, such a circuit should be called a Current-
Controlled Oscillator (CCO). However, in practice there is little
significant difference between VCOs and CCOs, and are entirely
interchangeable in virtually all applications. All electrically controlled oscillators are usually called VCOs.

Another name for VCOs that you may encounter, is "voltage-
to-frequency converter." Obviously, this is because the input voltage is converted into an analogous output frequency. A related type
of circuit is the frequency-to-voltage converter. As the name
suggests, this type of circuit works in just the opposite manner as
the voltage-to-frequency comparator—an input ac signal is
converted into a dc voltage at the output, which is proportional to
the input frequency. Many VCOs are also function generators,
offering multiple waveforms.

The term "voltage-controlled oscillator" is applied to any

electrically controllable signal generator circuit, whether or not it is a true oscillator.

A SIMPLE VCO CIRCUIT

Figure 7-1 shows a very simple VCO circuit built around a UJT (see Chapter 4). Notice that this circuit is essentially a variation on the basic UJT signal generator circuit.

One very unusual feature of this circuit should be apparent just by looking at the schematic. There is no power supply! The circuit is powered by the control voltage.

The output frequency is inversely proportional to the control voltage. That is, the higher the control voltage (providing, of course, that the maximum ratings of the transistor are not exceeded), the lower the output frequency is. Typically, for most UJTs, the usable range of input voltage is from about 5 to approximately 30 volts. Almost any general purpose UJT can be used in this circuit. The 2N2646 is a good choice.

Resistor R2's value should be approximately 100 ohms or so. This value is not at all critical. Anything close to 100 ohms may be used.

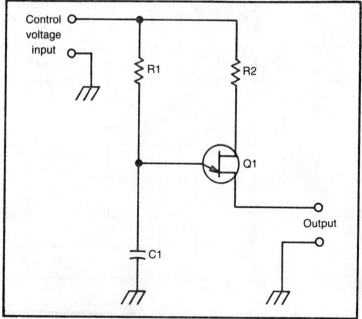

Fig. 7-1. A simple UJT VCO circuit.

Resistor R1 and capacitor C1 control the range of output frequencies. It is suggested that you breadboard this circuit and experiment with different values for these components. For best results, keep the value of R1 between 8.2 k and 62 k. The value of C1 should be between about 0.1 μF to 5 μF.

You can also experiment with this circuit by adding various components between the input and ground. A diode or a capacitor of about 100 μF produces particularly striking (and quite different) effects if the output is fed through an amplifier and loudspeaker.

MULTI-WAVEFORM VCO

A slightly more advanced VCO circuit is shown in Fig. 7-2. This circuit puts out three different waveforms simultaneously:

☐ An ascending sawtooth wave (output A, from the Collector of Q1)

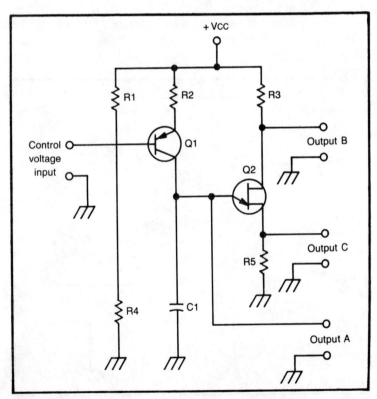

Fig. 7-2. This VCO can put out three simultaneous waveforms.

146

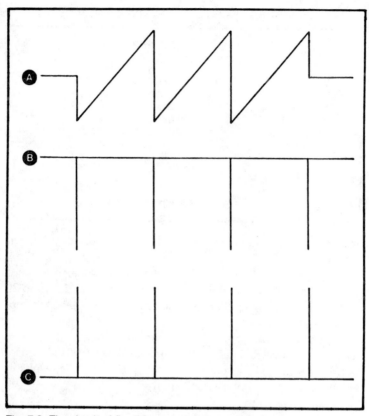

Fig. 7-3. The circuit of fig. 7-2 generates these waveshapes.

□ A negative spike wave (output B, from base 1 of Q2)
□ A positive spike wave (output C, from base 2 of Q2)

The three output waveshapes are illustrated in Fig. 7-3.

A partial parts list for this project is given in Table 7-1. None of the component values are particularly critical. Feel free to substitute nearby values, if you choose.

Resistor R2 and capacitor C1 are the components of most interest to us here, since they determine the range of output frequencies. The larger the values of these two components, the lower the base output frequency. For best results, R2 should be between 1 k and 22 k, and C1 should be between 0.001 μF to about 10 μF. The formula for the output frequency is:

$$F = (2/R2C1) \times [1 - (V1/V_{CC})]$$

147

Table 7-1. Partial Parts List for the VCO Circuit of Fig. 7-2.

Q1	2N1309 PNP
Q2	2N491 UJT
R1	330 K (330,000 ohms)
R2	see text
R3,R5	330 ohms
R4	1 Meg (1,000,000 ohms)
C1	see text
V_{cc}	18 volts to 24 volts

where VCC is the supply voltage, and V1 is the control voltage at the input.

This particular circuit works best with supply voltages between 18 volts and 24 volts, and input (control) voltages in the 10 to 20 volt range. The input voltage should always be less than the supply voltage.

For your calculations, assume a supply voltage of 22.5 volts. Also, assume that R2 is a 10 k resistor, and C1 is a 0.001 μF capacitor. In this example, a control voltage input of 10 volts results in an output frequency of approximately:

$$F = [2/(10000 \times 0.00000001)] \times [1 \times (10/22.5)]$$
$$= (2/0.00001) \times (1 - 0.4444)$$
$$= 200.000 \times 0.5556$$
$$= 111.111 \text{ Hz.}$$

If you raise the control voltage at the input to 15 volts, the output frequency becomes approximately:

$$F = 200.000 \times [1 - (15/22.5)]$$
$$= 200.000 \times (1 - 0.6667)$$
$$= 200.000 \times 0.3333$$
$$= 66.666 \text{ Hz}$$

Increasing the input voltage to 20 volts brings the output frequency down to about:

$$F = 200.000 \times (1 - (20/22.5))$$

$$= 200.000 \times (1 - 0.8889)$$
$$= 200.000 \times 0.1111$$
$$= 22.222 \text{ Hz}$$

Notice that as the control voltage at the input increases, the output frequency decreases.

Now, let's leave R2 and Vcc at their same values, but increase the value of C1 to 0.5 μF. Here are the resulting output frequencies for each of the control voltages used in the previous example:

Vi = 10 volts
F = [2/(10000 × 0.00000005)] × [1 − (10/22.5)]
  = (2/0.005) × (1 − 0.4444)
  = 400 × 0.5556
  = 222 Hz

Vi = 15 volts
F = 400 × [1 − (15/22.5)]
  = 400 × (1 − 0.6667)
  = 400 × 0.3333
  = 133 Hz

Vi = 20 volts
F = 400 × (1 − (20/22.5))
  = 400 × (1 − 0.8889)
  = 400 × 0.1111
  = 44 Hz

For the next example, increase the value of C1 to 10 μF, and perform the calculations once more:

F = [2/(10000 × 0.00001)] × [1 − (10/22.5)]
  = (2/0.1) × (1 − 0.4444)
  = 20 × 0.5556
  = 11 Hz

F = 20 × [1 − (15/22.5)]
  = 20 × (1 − 0.6667)
  = 20 × 0.3333
  = 6.7 Hz

F = 20 × (1 − (20/22.5)
  = 20 × (1 − 0.8889)

$$= 20 \times 0.1111$$
$$= 2.2 \text{ Hz}$$

Increasing the capacitance decreases the output frequency for a given input voltage. This same rule of thumb also applies for the value of R2. Increasing this resistance decreases the output frequency for a given input voltage.

In other words, increasing R2, C1, or Vi reduces the output frequency from this circuit.

SINE WAVE VCO

Most standard sine wave oscillators are difficult to convert to voltage-controlled operation, but some applications call for voltage-controlled sine waves. One example is the process of additive synthesis in electronic music systems.

One solution would be to use a waveform with relatively weak harmonics, like the triangle wave, and use a low-pass filter to delete the harmonics. For best results, the filter should be voltage-controlled too, because the harmonics that need to be removed will vary with the VCO's output frequency.

The problem is best illustrated with an example. Let's assume we have a triangle wave feeding through a low-pass filter with a cut-off frequency of 500 Hz. For convenience, we will only look at the harmonics up to the ninth.

If the VCO is generating a 300 Hz triangle wave, this system works as desired:

Harmonic	VCO	Filter
Fundamental	300 Hz	300 Hz
third	900 Hz	
fifth	1500 Hz	
seventh	2100 Hz	
ninth	2700 Hz	

But if you lower the VCO's output frequency to 110 Hz, some of the lower harmonics get through the filter:

Harmonic	VCO	Filter
Fundamental	110 Hz	110 Hz
third	330 Hz	330 Hz

fifth	550 Hz	(550 Hz?)
seventh	770 Hz	
ninth	990 Hz	

The fifth harmonic will probably appear in the filter's output, even though it is higher than the cut-off frequency. No filter has an infinitely sharp cut-off. The fifth harmonic in this case is attenuated, but not deleted entirely.

The problem is even worse if we lower the VCO frequency further:

Harmonic	VCO	Filter
Fundamental	60 Hz	60 Hz
third	180 Hz	180 Hz
fifth	300 Hz	300 Hz
seventh	420 Hz	420 Hz
ninth	540 Hz	(540 Hz)

And what happens if you raise the VCO's output frequency above 500 Hz (the cut-off frequency of the filter)? There may be no signal at the output at all. A fixed cut-off frequency filter is only adequate for a fairly narrow range of frequencies.

It is possible to build a VCO that generates sine waves directly. One such circuit is shown in Fig. 7-4. (The parts list is given in Table 7-2.)

OP AMP VCO

Yet another useful VCO circuit is shown in Fig. 7-5. (The parts list is given in Table 7-3.) The main active components in this rather simple circuit are an op amp and a SCR. Of the circuits presented in this chapter so far, this one is probably the most suitable for electronic music applications.

One simple improvement on this circuit is to add a range switch. Use a rotary switch to select one of several values for capacitor C1. The capacitance values should be kept between about 0.01 μF and 1 μF.

Another simple improvement is to add a fine tuning control. Simply replace resistor R3 with a 2.2 k resistor and a 10 k potentiometer.

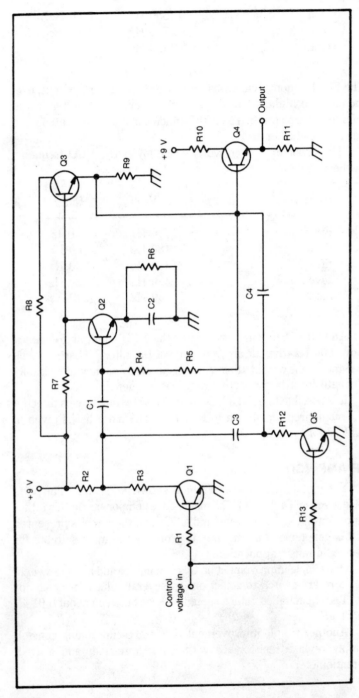

Fig. 7-4. A voltage-controlled sine wave oscillator circuit.

Table 7-2. A Partial Parts List for the VCO Circuit of Fig. 7-4.

R1, R13	470 Ω resistor
R2, R12	560 Ω resistor
R3, R4, R9	8.2 kΩ resistor
R5	1 kΩ resistor
R6	420 Ω resistor
R7	2.2 kΩ resistor
R8, R11	4.7 kΩ resistor
R10	100 Ω resistor
C1	0.047 μF capacitor
C2	1 μF capacitor
C3	0.01 μF capacitor
C4	0.022 μF capacitor
Q1-Q5	NPN transistor (2N4264, GE-17, Motorola HEP-50, or Radio Shack RS-2016)

VOLTAGE-TO-FREQUENCY CONVERSION

As stated earlier, a VCO is often called a voltage-to-frequency converter. Strictly speaking, there are some minor differences between VCOs and voltage-to-frequency converters, but the circuits are closely related.

This section considers the specifics of the voltage to-frequency converter.

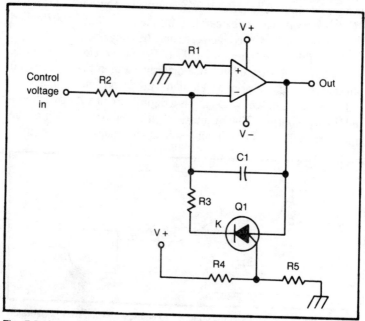

Fig. 7-5. An op amp can also be used to build a VCO.

Table 7-3. Recommended Component Values for the VCO Circuit of Fig. 7-5.

R1-R3, R5	10 kΩ resistor
R4	3.3 kΩ resistor
C1	0.15 μF capacitor
Q1	SCR (2N6027, or equivalent)
IC1	op amp IC (741, or equivalent)

In many applications, it is to transmit electrical information, such as voltages, from one place to another, or to record it for later recovery. This is fairly easy to accomplish when the data to be recorded is made up of ac signals in the audible range (approximately 50 Hz to 15 kHz). Such signals can be transmitted directly over telephone lines, or recorded using standard audio tape recorders.

For dc or near-dc signals (close to 0 Hz) the normal limitations of the audio circuits get in the way. One common approach to solving this type of problem is the convert the dc or very low frequency signals into higher frequency signals that can be more readily transmitted and/or recorded. The frequency of the new ac signal corresponds directly to the instantaneous voltage of the dc or near-dc input voltage. This is accomplished with a VCO. When VCOs are used to encode dc or low-frequency data, they are called Voltage-to-Frequency converters, or V/F converters.

One of the simplest approaches to V/F conversion is the single slope method, illustrated in block diagram form in Fig. 7-6. As you can see, the circuit's primary elements are an op amp comparator, and an AND gate. An AND gate is a digital circuit with two inputs and a single output. The output is high if and only if both of the inputs are high. Any other input combination results in a low output.

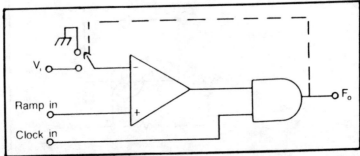

Fig. 7-6. One of the simplest approaches to voltage-to-frequency conversion is the single slope method.

154

An external sawtooth or ramp signal is required. The voltage to be converted (Vi) is fed to the inverting input of the op amp comparator. At the same time, the reference ramp signal is fed to the non-inverting input.

In practical circuits, the switch shown here as S1 is electronically controlled. It is shown here as a manual switch for simplicity. At time T0, the switch is in the grounded position. Zero volts is applied to the inverting input. The ramp signal voltage also begins at zero volts. Since the inputs to the comparator are equal, the output is low. This means the AND gate will be closed (output low) regardless of the current value of the incoming clock pulses.

The ramp begins to rise from zero. As soon as it is a few millivolts above zero, the comparator's output snaps to the positive saturation state (high). This feeds a logic 1 to the AND gate, allowing the clock pulses to pass through to the output. Remember, the output of an AND gate is high if and only if both of its inputs are high. The signals in the circuit look like this:

Comparator Output	Clock	AND Gate Output
LOW	LOW	LOW
LOW	HIGH	LOW
HIGH	LOW	LOW
HIGH	HIGH	HIGH

When the comparator output is high, the AND gate's output is the same as the clock. At the same time, switch S1 reverses its position, and starts feeding Vi to the inverting input of the comparator.

When the ramp voltage equals or exceeds Vi, the comparator's output goes low again, cutting off the AND gate, and the stream of clock pulses to the output.

Switch S1 now moves back to its grounded position, and the ramp voltage drops back to zero. The cycle now begins again. A typical cycle is illustrated in Fig. 7-7. The number of output pulses between times T0 and T1 is proportional to the input voltage.

While some F/V converters are basically VCOs, this one is not. It does not even perform true voltage-to-frequency conversion. The output frequency (the rate of the clock pulses) is constant. The higher the level of Vi, the longer the AND gate will be open, permitting more clock pulses to reach the output during the cycle.

155

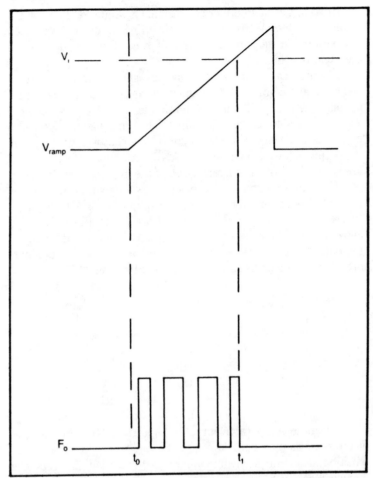

Fig. 7-7. A typical cycle for a single slope voltage-to-frequency converter.

This signal can easily be decoded with a digital counting circuit. A digital-to-analog (D/A) converter can be used to convert the digital count back into an analog voltage to recreate the original signal.

This single slope approach to frequency-to-voltage conversion is limited primarily by the accuracy and linearity of the ramp waveform, and the consistency of the clock rate. This type of circuit also tends to be susceptible to interference errors due to noise.

Better results can be obtained with a dual slope V/F converter. This process is shown in block diagram form in Fig. 7-8. Once again this is actually only pseudo V/F conversion. The level of the input voltage-controls the number of constant frequency output pulses.

Notice that two op amp stages are required for this type of circuit. IC1 is wired as an integrator, and IC2 is wired as a comparator.

At time T0, the input voltage to be measured is applied to the integrator (IC1) through switch S1. The integrator capacitor is charged at a fairly linear rate until Vi is removed (by S1), or reversed in polarity. The instant that the voltage across this capacitor rises above zero, the output of the comparator snaps to its high state, and turns on the AND gate, permitting the clock pulses to reach the output, as in the single slope circuit. This switching action happens almost immediately.

A digital counter is incremented by the train of clock pulses at the output of the AND gate. Eventually, the counter's maximum count is exceeded. The overflow signal is fed back to electronic switch S1, toggling it to the VREF (constant reference voltage) position. This occurs at time T1.

The reference voltage is supplied by a constant current voltage source with a polarity the opposite that of Vi. When this voltage is applied to the input of the integrator, the capacitor starts to discharge. The clock pulses meanwhile continue incrementing the counter. (The counter starts over at 0000 when it overflows.)

When the capacitor is completely discharged, the voltage across it is zero (or slightly negative). The comparator output goes low, and the AND gate is closed, cutting off the flow of clock pulses

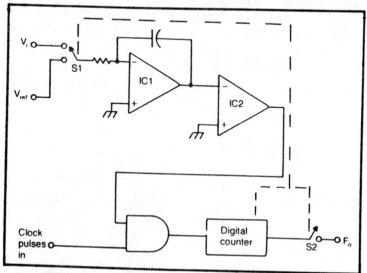

Fig. 7-8. Better voltage-to-frequency conversion can be achieved with a dual slope circuit.

to the counter. This happens at time T2. The number of pulses between times T1 and T2 is directly proportional to the level of input voltage Vi. Switch S2 is used to isolate the output from time T0 to T1, when the preliminary count is being performed.

Both the single slope and dual slope circuits are frequently encountered in digital voltmeters and related instruments, as well as in communications and recording systems.

The circuit shown in Fig. 7-9 performs true voltage-to-frequency conversion. At time T0, switch S1 is open, and capacitor C1 is fully discharged. The input voltage to be converted (Vi) is fed to the non-inverting input of the comparator (IC1). As soon as Vi is even slightly greater than zero, the comparator output goes HIGH, triggering the monostable multivibrator. This also closes switch S1, permitting the reference voltage (VREF—a precise constant-current source) to start charging capacitor C1. S1 is held closed for a fixed time interval determined by the time constant of resistor R2 and capacitor C2.

After the monostable multivibrator times out (the timing cycle ends), one of two things can happen. If the charge across capacitor C1 is greater than the input voltage (Vi), the comparator's output goes low, and the monostable multivibrator is not retriggered. If, on the other hand, Vi is still greater than the charge on capacitor C1, the comparator's output remains high, immediately retriggering the monostable multivibrator for another fixed time period. This gives VREF more time to charge capacitor C1. This continues until C1 is charged to a higher voltage than Vi. The effect of all this is to create an output pulse whose width is roughly proportional to the input voltage (Vi), as illustrated in Fig. 7-10.

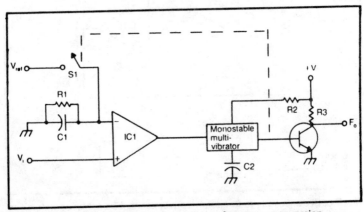

Fig. 7-9. This circuit performs true voltage-to-frequency conversion.

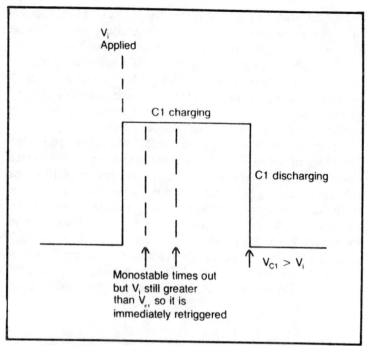

Fig. 7-10. The monostable multivibrator in the circuit of Fig. 7-9 generates an output pulse whose width is roughly proportional to the input voltage.

When the monostable multivibrator is no longer being retriggered, the output goes LOW, and capacitor C1 begins to discharge through resistor R1. At some point, the voltage across this capacitor drops below Vi, causing the charging cycle to begin again.

In effect, the length of each charging cycle, and the interval between them is directly dependent on the amplitude of Vi. The higher the voltage, the longer it takes the capacitor to charge and discharge. In other words, increasing the input voltage reduces the number of cycles that occur per second. Raising the input voltage decreases the output frequency proportionately.

The opposite action—i.e., converting a frequency into a proportional dc voltage—is performed by a Frequency-to-Voltage (F/V) converter. The specific circuitry for F/V converters is beyond the scope of this book.

VCOS AND ELECTRONIC MUSIC

VCOs are used in many applications. (Many involve PLLs, discussed in Chapter 8.) One important class of VCO applications lies in the area of electronic music. To produce musical tones electronically, an oscillator is used as the original tone source.

Composing and performing music on a manually controlled oscillator would be extremely tedious at best. Early avant garde electronic composers often spent weeks or even months putting together a taped piece that might run a minute or two. Live performances were virtually out of the question.

Electronic music did not become popular until the sixties when Bob Moog introduced his first modular synthesizer that was built around the then revolutionary concept of voltage-control. Electrical voltages set the signal parameters much more accurately and far faster than any human operator could ever manage by twiddling knobs. Much of the work involved in sound synthesis can be automated by voltage-control.

Many of the newer digital synthesizers feature DCOs or digitally controlled oscillators. A DCO is nothing more than the software equivalent of a VCO, used in exactly the same manner as a VCO.

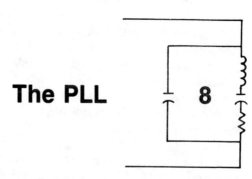

The PLL   8

CLOSELY RELATED TO THE VCO IS THE PLL, OR PHASE-LOCKED loop. If you have been involved with electronics at all in the last few years, you have undoubtably heard the term, although you may be a little unclear about just what it means. If so, don't feel too bad. A lot of experienced technicians still feel quite hazy when it comes to PLLs.

There is really no reason for all the confusion. Somehow the phase-locked loop has acquired an undeserved reputation for being a very mysterious and esoteric device. Many technicians feel the PLL is best left to the experts, but are afraid to try to become experts themselves. There is really no need for this attitude. The PLL isn't particularly difficult to master with a little effort.

WHAT IS A PLL?

Like the operational amplifier, the phase-locked loop's operation is based on the principle of feedback. The op amp normally feeds back voltages (or sometimes, currents), while the PLL feeds back ac frequencies.

A simplified block diagram of a phase-locked loop is shown in Fig. 8-1. As you can see, it is made up of three major parts:

- ☐ A phase detector
- ☐ a low-pass filter
- ☐ a VCO (voltage-controlled oscillator)

The phase detector has two inputs, the input to the PLL as a whole, and the feedback output of the PLL. Both signals are ac frequencies. These two frequencies are compared to determine if they are in phase with each other. If they are, the phase detector puts out no error signal, and everything is fine.

But if the signals are not in phase, a voltage proportional to the amount of the phase difference (or error) appears at the output of the phase detector stage. Obviously, if the two signals do not have exactly identical frequencies, they aren't going to be able to stay in phase with each other for more than a fraction of a second. In a very real sense, the phase detector not only detects differences in phase, it also detects differences in frequency. The greater the phase (or frequency) difference is between the input and feedback signals, the greater the error voltage. The error signal can be either positive or negative.

The low-pass filter simply cleans up the error signal somewhat for smoother operation. Without the filter, (which is omitted in some very inexpensive PLL circuits) brief bursts of noise can cause false error signals to make the PLL behave erratically. With the low-pass filter included, only relatively low speed errors (such as those caused by oscillator drift) get through. These are the error signals of insignificance in a phase-locked loop.

The final stage, the VCO, is not dissimilar to the circuits described in Chapter 7. In the PLL, the error signal is used as the control voltage. If the output frequency of the VCO is too low for any reason, the phase detector puts out an error signal that is fed to the control input of the VCO, forcing it to raise its frequency. Similarly, if the VCO's output frequency goes too high, the error signal from the phase detector forces the VCO's frequency back down to the desired point. If the VCO is putting out exactly the right output (correct frequency and correct phase), there is no error

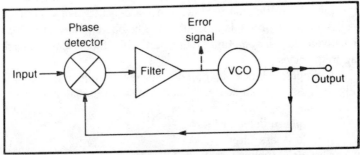

Fig. 8-1. A phase-locked loop is made up of three primary sections.

162

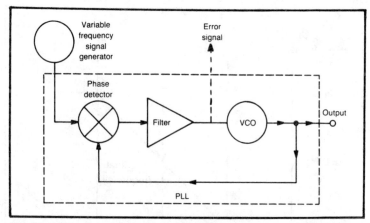

Fig. 8-2. The text explores what happens when a variable frequency signal generator is connected to the input of a PLL.

signal from the phase detector, so there is no control voltage to the VCO forcing it to alter its frequency in either direction.

In other words, the phase-locked loop is used to create a self-correcting ac frequency. That's all there is to it. It's not really so complicated, is it?

THE PLL IN ACTION

To get a clearer picture of the PLL, let's take a look at one in operation. This discussion is based on the block diagram shown in Fig. 8-2. This is the basic PLL block diagram that was presented earlier, with a variable frequency signal generator connected to the input. Notice that the error voltage can be tapped off after the filter stage. This is very useful or even essential in certain applications.

The VCO stage generates square waves (true of most modern PLLs in IC form). The nominal (no control voltage) frequency of the VCO in our example is 1000 Hz. The control voltage can force the output frequency up to 100 Hz in either direction. The operation of this VCO is illustrated in Fig. 8-3.

When the control voltage (error signal) is 0, the VCO puts out its nominal frequency of 1000 Hz. The output frequency linearly increases as the control/error voltage is made more positive. The output frequency increases 10 Hz per volt. Such increases go up to a limit of +10 volts, at which point the VCO is putting out its maximum frequency (1100 Hz). Similarly, the output frequency

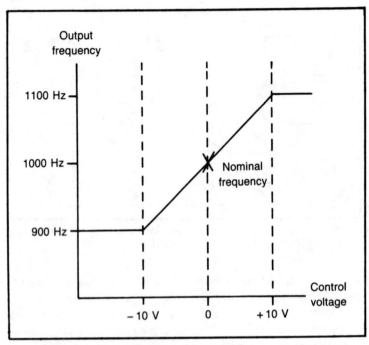

Fig. 8-3. The operation of the PLL's internal VCO.

smoothly decreases as the control/error voltage is made more negative. With a control/error voltage of – 10 volts, the VCO puts out its minimum frequency (900 Hz). If the signal generator is not connected to the input of the VCO, the output is the VCO's nominal 1000 Hz square wave.

Now, if the signal generator is connected to the input of the VCO and set for a frequency of about 700 Hz, how will this affect the PLL's output? Well, as it turns out, there is very little effect. The difference frequency is high enough so that most of the error signal is removed by the filter. No control voltage to speak of reaches the VCO, so it just perks along, more or less at its nominal frequency.

If the frequency from the signal generator is slowly increased, the output frequency of the PLL starts to become somewhat unstable. The output signal "jitters." The difference frequency is now becoming low enough to get through the filter and Frequency Modulate the output of the VCO around its nominal frequency.

When the input signal exceeds approximately 900 Hz, the VCO's output suddenly jumps to a stable frequency equal to that of the signal generator. The VCO remains locked to the input frequency, as long as the input frequency remains within the VCO's range. If the input frequency changes (as long as it remains in range), the output of the PLL follows it exactly. If the input signal goes significantly outside the VCO's range, the output snaps back to the nominal frequency.

Let's say the input and output signals are locked at 950 Hz. Now, suppose the VCO frequency tries to drift upwards for some reason—perhaps in response to a change in the ambient temperature. It doesn't have to change much; just a fraction of a hertz alters the phase relationship between the input and output signals enough to be noticed by the phase detector stage. The phase detector produces an error signal proportional to the change in the VCO's output frequency. This error signal is fed to the control input of the VCO, changing its frequency by a proportional, but opposite amount. This brings it right back to the desired frequency (950 Hz in our example). Any errors in the output frequency are self-correcting.

SOME TYPICAL PLL ICS

Today most PLL are in IC form. A number of such devices have been made available. This section looks at just a few typical examples.

The LM565, a popular general purpose phase-locked loop IC,

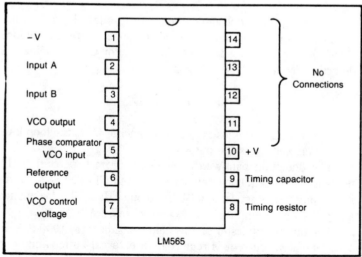

Fig. 8-4. The LM565 is a popular PLL IC.

is illustrated in Fig. 8-4. The 565 features a double balanced phase detector which offers good carrier suppression. The VCO in this chip is very stable, and highly linear. This allows the LM565 to be used to low distortion FM demodulation applications. The nominal frequency of the VCO can be set with an external resistor and capacitor, a wide tuning range (10:1) can be achieved with a single resistor. Such important characteristics as bandwidth, response speed, capture range, and pull-in range, are set with an external resistor and capacitor. The feedback loop between the VCO and the phase detector can be broken to allow the addition of a digital frequency divider to make the LM565 capable of frequency multiplication and frequency synthesis applications.

A closely related device is the LM567 tone decoder, shown in Fig. 8-5. A tone decoder is a variant form of the basic PLL. This type of circuit responds to a specific frequency or tone, while ignoring all others.

There are many potential applications for tone decoders including:

☐ Automatic paging systems
☐ Communications systems
☐ Electronic locks
☐ Intrusion alarms
☐ Radio controlled garage door openers
☐ Radio controlled model airplanes

The basic tone decoder circuit built around the 567 is not complex. Only a handful of external components are required, as shown in Fig. 8-6. Resistor R1 and capacitor C1 determine the detected frequency. The formula is:

$$F = 1.1/(R1C1)$$

Resistor R2 is the load resistor. Capacitor C2 is the loop low-pass filter, and C3 is the output filter.

The detection bandwidth can be set from 0 percent to 14 percent of the frequency defined by R1 and C1. The 567 can be set for any frequency from 0.01 Hz to 500 kHz, and it locks onto a signal with an amplitude as low as 20 mV RMS.

The output transistor on this chip can sink up to 1000 mA. If a larger output current is required, an external buffer amplifier stage should be used.

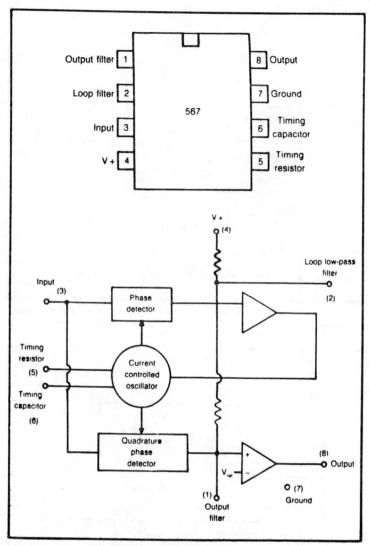

Fig. 8-5. A tone decoder, like the LM567 IC, is a variant of the basic PLL.

The 567 can be powered by a voltage source anywhere from 4.75 to 9 volts. Current consumption without a load is only 11 to 15 mA. The standby current consumption is a mere 6 to 10 mA while activated.

A demonstration circuit for the LM567 tone decoder is illustrated in Fig. 8-7. A typical parts list is given in Table 8-1. With the component values given here, the 567 (IC2) detects a frequency

167

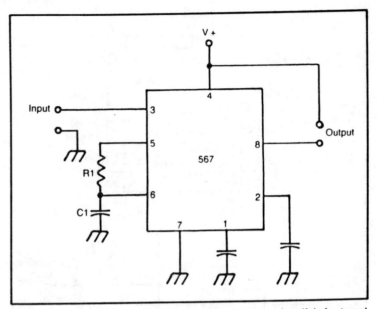

Fig. 8-6. The basic 567 tone decoder circuit requires just a handful of external components.

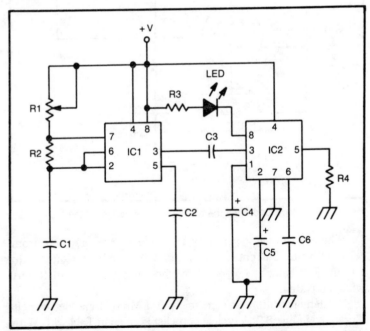

Fig. 8-7. This circuit demonstrates the operation of the 567 tone decoder.

168

IC1	555 timer
IC2	567 tone decoder
C1	0.05 μF capacitor
C2	0.01 μF capacitor
C3	0.1 μF capacitor
C4	2.2 μF capacitor
C5	1 μF capacitor
C6	0.02 μF capacitor
R1	10 k potentiometer
R2, R3	1 k resistor
R4	10 k resistor

of about 5000 Hz. IC1 is a 555 timer set up as an astable multivibrator (discussed back in Chapter 6). This is simply a built-in tone source. The generated tone is controlled by potentiometer R4. When the 555 produces a frequency in the 567's detection range, the LED lights.

This is just a demonstration circuit with no practical purpose, but it can be readily adapted for practical applications. Eliminating the 555 and its associated components allow you to use almost any signal source as the input to this circuit. Any reasonably low-current output device can be used in place of the LED.

Figure 8-8 shows the pinout diagram for two more popular PLL ICs, the LM1391 and the LM1394. The only difference between the two is the polarity of the phase detector.

These ICs were designed specifically for use in the horizontal section of television sets, but there's no reason why they can't be used in other low frequency signal processing applications.

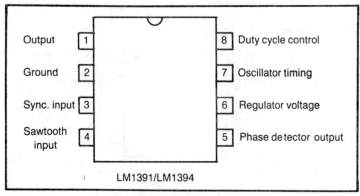

Fig. 8-8. The LM1391 and LM1394 PLL ICs have the same pinout.

The LM1391 and LM1394 include a linear pulse phase detector, a highly stable VCO, an a variable duty cycle (variable pulse width) output driver.

The LM1310, shown in Fig. 8-9, is a more specialized phase-locked loop IC. This device is designed for use in FM stereo demodulation. It uses PLL techniques to regenerate the 38 kHz subcarrier. This chip offers excellent channel separation and automatic switching between stereo and mono modes. Unlike most other FM stereo demodulation circuits available today, a circuit built around the LM1310 requires no bulky and expensive coils. All tuning is accomplished with just a single potentiometer. The LM1310 delivers high fidelity sound, but is inexpensive enough to be used even in low cost stereo equipment.

A close relative of the LM1310 is the LM1800, which offers the same features already mentioned, in addition to excellent power supply rejection, the LM1800 also features buffered outputs to the basic PLL decoder circuit.

APPLICATIONS

What is a phase-locked loop good for? Many applications take advantage of the unique characteristics of the PLL

A PLL can lock on to a relatively low level signal even if there is a lot of random noise that may actually be greater than the desired signal itself. The noise pulses are probably outside the VCO's range,

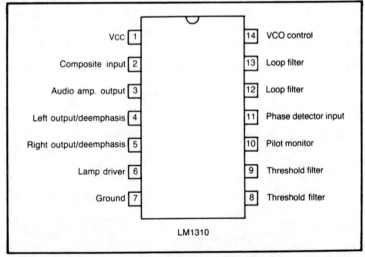

Fig. 8-9. The LM310 PLL IC was designed for use in FM stereo demodulation.

so they are effectively ignored. This makes the PLL highly usefully as a CW amplifier and noise filter.

The PLL responds to only a specific range, or band of frequencies, so it can be used as a modified band-pass amplifier.

One of the most common applications for PLLs is in FM demodulation. If the i-f (Intermediate Frequency) is used as the center frequency of the VCO, and the FM signal is used as the PLL's input, tapping off the error signal at the output of the filter stage will reproduce the modulating program signal.

Phase-locked loops are also widely used in applications involving the transmission and/or storage of digitally encoded data. Digital signals consist of just two specific levels (1 and 0). These two levels can be represented by two specific frequencies for transmission over telephone lines, or for storage on an audio tape recorder. This technique is known as frequency shift keying, or FSK. A PLL can be used to decode the FSK data. The logic 1 frequency is slightly higher than the nominal frequency of the PLL's VCO. The logic 0 is slightly less than the VCO's nominal frequency.

FSK data is decoded at the error signal output, after the filter stage. If this signal is positive, the circuit has received a logic 1. If this signal is negative, it has received a logic 0. If no signal is currently being recovered, the error signal is zero, and the VCO is operating at its nominal frequency.

PLLs are also frequently employed for data synchronization applications. In many computer and other digital systems, two or more circuits must have clock signals to drive them. The various devices must all use the same clock signal, or synchronized clock signals to prevent them from getting out of step with each other. If the various sub-circuits in a digital system get out of synchronization, the data being transmitted back and forth between them gets hopelessly scrambled. A PLL data synchronizer circuit eliminates the need for an independent transmission line just for the clock signal.

Another popular application for phase-locked loops is motor speed control. The input signal in this case comes from a tachometer monitoring the speed of the motor.

PLLs are also widely used for frequency synthesis. PLL frequency synthesizers become popular when the CB (Citizens Band) radio service was expanded to 40 channels, and multi-crystal tuning systems were no longer practical.

A block diagram for a typical PLL frequency synthesis circuit is shown in Fig. 8-10. By selecting the right frequency for the crystal

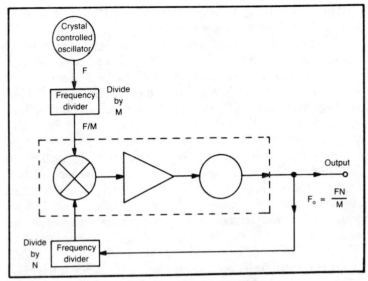

Fig. 8-10. PLLs are often used for frequency synthesis.

controlled oscillator, and the proper values for the frequency divider stages, virtually any desired frequency can appear the output of the PLL.

Notice that the oscillator frequency is divided by M before it reaches the PLL. A second frequency divider stage (divide by N) is placed in the VCO's feedback path. The output frequency equals:

$$Fo = FN/M$$

F is the original frequency generated by the crystal controlled oscillator.

To show how this works try a simple example. Assume that the original oscillator frequency is 3.58 MHz. The first frequency divider (M) divides by 500. The second frequency divider (N) divides by 12. The output frequency is therefore equal to:

$$\begin{aligned} Fo &= (3580000 \times 12)/500 \\ &= 42960000/500 \\ &= 85920 \text{ Hz} \\ &= 85.92 \text{ kHz} \end{aligned}$$

As you can see, the phase-locked loop isn't really all that complicated. The PLL is a very versatile and useful device.

Digital
Signal Generators

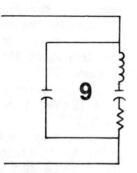

9

DIGITAL CIRCUITS HAVE JUST TWO POSSIBLE SIGNAL LEVELS, high (1), and low (0). In a sense, all digital signals are more or less modified rectangle waves. This suggests that there should be no problem in generating periodic rectangle waves and square waves by purely digital means.

Furthermore, as you will learn later in this chapter, a little ingenuity also lets you generate almost any waveform digitally.

CLOCK PULSE GENERATORS

All sequential digital logic systems require at least one clock pulse generator. A clock pulse generator is simply an appropriate square wave generator. Occasionally, a rectangle wave with a duty cycle other than 1:2 may be used.

Many popular microprocessors feature built-in clock pulse generators. Other sequential digital systems may use clocks made from 555 timers, a pair of cross-coupled inverters, or a trio of inverters connected as a ring oscillator.

A number of simple but useful digitally clocking circuits can be built around a handful of simple inverters. An inverter is a digital device with a single input and a single output. The output is always in the opposite state as the input. That is, if the input is high, the output is low, and if the input is low, then the output is high. That is all that an inverter does. This wouldn't seem to be a very likely candidate for signal generation. But by using feedback, a series of inverters can generate a fine rectangle wave.

A typical circuit is shown in Fig. 9-1. This circuit is made up of three TTL inverters (half of a 7405 hex inverter IC), three resistors, and a capacitor. Because the 7405 contains six independent inverter sections, two of these circuits could be built around a single IC. This circuit can be built around any of the TTL subfamilies, such as the 74L05, 74H05, 74LS05, or whatever.

The 7405 hex inverter is used in this circuit, instead of the somewhat more common 7404 IC, because the 7405 has open collector outputs. The circuit may not function properly if a 7404 is substituted.

The output frequency of this circuit is approximately 1 MHz to 10 MHz, depending on the value of R, which is normally in about 1 k to 4 k.

Another inverter-based clock pulse generator circuit is shown in Fig. 9-2. This circuit is built around a pair of CMOS inverters (1/3 of a CD4049 hex inverter IC). The unused inverter inputs should be grounded to ensure stability. Of course, the extra inverters could be put to work in other circuitry.

This circuit is extremely small. Only two external components are required in addition to the IC itself: a resistor and a capacitor. These two discrete components determine the output clock frequency. The capacitor's value should be kept in the 0.01 μF to

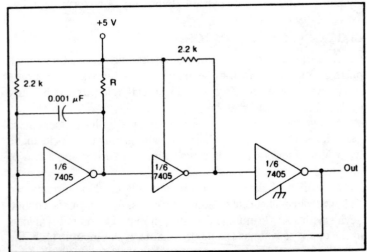

Fig. 9-1. A simple clock pulse generator circuit can be made from three TTL inverters.

174

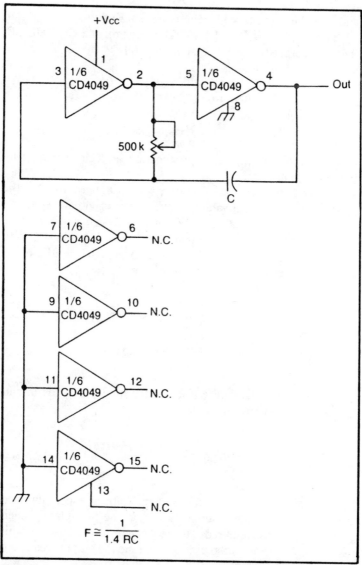

Fig. 9-2. Two CMOS inverters are at the heart of this clock pulse generator circuit.

10 μF range. The formula for the output frequency is:

$$F = 1/(1.4RC)$$

F is the output frequency hertz, R is the resistance in megohms, and C is the capacitance in microfarads (μF).

For example, if R = 1 k (0.001 megohm), and C = 0.01 μF, then the output frequency is approximately:

$$
\begin{aligned}
F &= 1/(1.4 \times 0.001 \times 0.01) \\
&= 1/0.000014 \\
&= 71500 \text{ Hz} \\
&= 71.5 \text{ kHz}
\end{aligned}
$$

This equation is only an approximation, especially with wide tolerance components.

In most practical applications, you will need to find the appropriate component values to give a specific output frequency.

For example, let's say you need to design a clock pulse generator with an output frequency of 5 kHz. The first step is to arbitrarily select a likely capacitance value—0.022 μF. Next, algebraically rearrange the equation to solve for R:

$$
\begin{aligned}
R &= 1/(1.4FC) \\
&= 1/(1.4 \times 5000 \times 0.022) \\
&= 1/154 \\
&= 0.0064935 \text{ megohms} \\
&= 6.5 \text{ k}
\end{aligned}
$$

If you use a standard 6.8 k resistor for R, then the output frequency is approximately:

$$
\begin{aligned}
F &= 1/(1.4 \times 0.0065 \times 0.022) \\
&= 1/0.0002002 \\
&= 4995 \text{ Hz}
\end{aligned}
$$

This should be close enough for most applications, especially since the equations are only approximations in the first place. When greater precision is required, a trimpot can be placed in series with resistor R. This allows the user to fine tune the output frequency as desired.

A fairly similar circuit is illustrated in Fig. 9-3. Here two CMOS NAND gates (half of a CD4011) are used in the place of the inverters. A second resistor is also added to the circuit. Typically, the capacitor in this circuit has a value somewhere between 0.01 μF and 0.1 μF. Resistor R2 is between about 10 k and 1 megohm. Resistor R1's value should be about 5 to 10 times the value of R2. R2 can be replaced with a potentiometer for a variable frequency

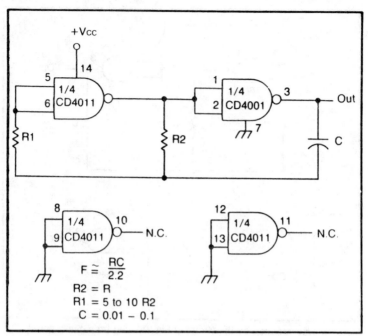

Fig. 9-3. NAND gates can be used in place of inverters in a clock pulse generator.

clock. The approximate output frequency for this circuit is:

$$F = RC/2.2$$

Once again, this equation is just an approximation. Here are some typical component values for this circuit. Note that any given frequency can be generated with various different combinations of component values:

F	R1	R2	C
45 Hz	68 k	10 k	0.01 μF
450 Hz	680 k	100 k	0.01 μF
4.5 kHz	10 Meg	1 Meg	0.01 μF
450 Hz	68 k	10 k	0.1 μF
2 kHz	330 k	47 k	0.1 μF
4.5 kHz	680 k	100 k	0.1 μF
21.4 kHz	3.3 Meg	470 k	0.1 μF
45 kHz	10 Meg	1 Meg	0.1 μF

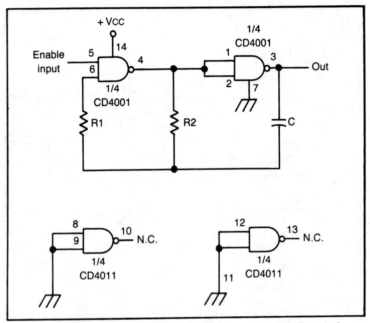

Fig. 9-4. This variation on the circuit of Fig. 9-3 can be digitally gated.

An interesting variation on this circuit is shown in Fig. 9-4. One of the NAND gate inputs can be externally controlled. Any digital signal can turn the clock on and off. A logic 0 (low) at the input inhibits the signal generator's operation, while a logic 1 (high) enables it. Such a gated clock can come in quite handy in many advanced circuits.

NOR gates can also be used to create digital clocking circuits. A typical circuit is shown in Fig. 9-5. This is a very precise circuit, thanks to the use of the crystal. Of course, the crystal is the primary factor in determining the output frequency. Varying the value of capacitor C (typically from 4 pF to 40 pF) permits some minor fine tuning of the output frequency for precision applications.

The component values indicated in the schematic were selected for peak performance around 1 MHz. For other output frequencies, you might want to experiment with other component values to get the cleanest possible output signal.

DEDICATED CLOCK ICS

Intersil makes a general purpose timer chip called the ICM7209. This IC has extraordinary specifications for a CMOS device. It is guaranteed to oscillate at frequencies up to 10 MHz, and can directly drive as many as 5 TTL gates (Fig. 9-6).

Like most CMOS devices, the ICM7209 is very power efficient. With a 5 V power supply, the chip typically consumes a mere 11 mA. Power dissipation of the ICM7209 is directly related to its oscillation frequency. Since the oscillator portion of the chip consumes much less power than its output buffers, power dissipation can be dramatically reduced when the chip is disabled by making pin 3 low. The oscillator portion continues to operate, but the output buffers are disabled, thus reducing their current drain.

This device operates with a minimum of three external components, two capacitors and a quartz crystal. The basic circuit is shown in Fig. 9-7.

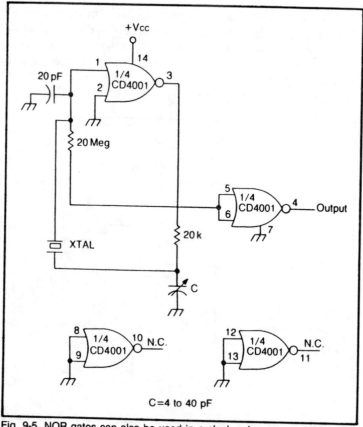

Fig. 9-5. NOR gates can also be used in a clock pulse generator circuit.

179

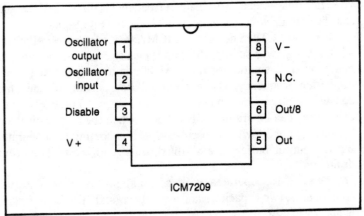

Fig. 9-6. The ICM7209 is a general purpose clock timer IC.

The crystal can be any quartz crystal having a resonant frequency of 10 kHz to 10 MHz. For best results, the crystal should have a load capacitance of 10 pF, rather than the usual 30 pF. When C1 and C2 each have a value of 18 pF this provides a typical frequency stability of 1 ppm per one volt change in the supply voltage. The circuit can be powered by a dc supply of 3 to 6 volts. The

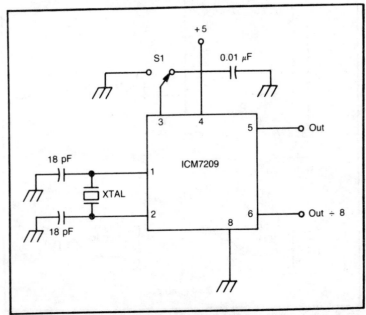

Fig. 9-7. Basic clock circuit using the ICM7209.

ICM7209 has 2 output pins. The divide-by-eight output (pin #6) can be used to obtain many combinations.

In the circuit shown in Fig. 9-7, the disable input (pin #3) is controlled by a switch. If you prefer, external logic circuitry could be used instead. Pin #3 can also be connected to either the oscillator in or out pins for some very interesting results. For example, if pin #3 is connected to pin #2 (in), each of the divide-by-eight pulses appearing at pin #6 are further divided into four separate pulses. This provides a burst output mode.

This particular oscillator circuit is not tunable, but the output frequency can easily be changed by simply replacing the crystal.

DIGITAL SYNTHESIS

While digital circuits can directly produce only rectangle waves, combining multiple rectangle waves in the proper way permits digital synthesis of virtually any imaginable waveform. To understand how this is done, let's briefly review analog-to-digital (A/D) and digital-to-analog (D/A) conversion.

At any given instant, you can express the current amplitude numerically. In A/D converters, this is called a sample. By taking several samples throughout the cycle, you can store the waveshape as a string of numbers, as illustrated in Fig. 9-8. The more samples

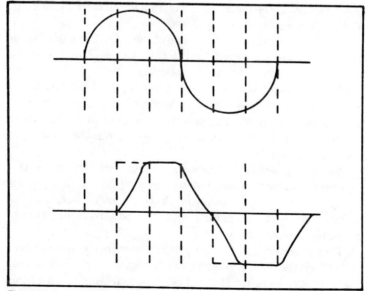

Fig. 9-8. A waveshape can be stored as a string of digital values.

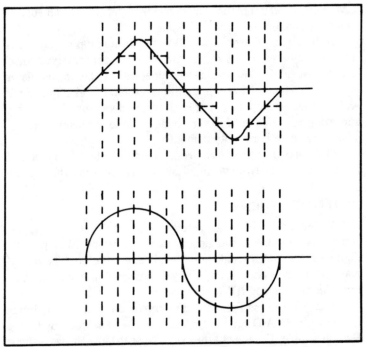

Fig. 9-9. The more samples taken per cycle, the better the resolution.

taken per cycle, the better the resolution of the stored waveform. This is demonstrated in Fig. 9-9.

D/A conversion is the other side of the coin. The stored string of numbers are converted back into a string of instantaneous voltages to recreate the analog waveform.

One disadvantage is that all of the re-created waveforms are filled with sharp edges. This problem can be greatly reduced by passing the re-created waveform through a low-pass filter. Often just a large capacitor is used. This smooths out the corners, as illustrated in Fig. 9-10.

Since any series of numbers can be fed through a D/A converter, you are not restricted to re-creating waveforms that have been stored via an A/D converter. A computer, for example, can be programmed to generate a repeating pattern of numbers to synthesize almost any waveform.

Digital synthesis is becoming more and more common. Deluxe radio receivers often feature digital tuning. Almost all electronic music synthesizers on the market today are digital synthesis devices.

182

True digital synthesis belongs in the realm of the computer and the microprocessor, which are beyond the scope of this book. But it is possible to build dedicated circuits that use the same fundamental principles. Such circuits are covered in the next few pages of this chapter.

DIGITAL FUNCTION GENERATORS

Figure 9-11 shows a block diagram for a typical programmable function generator. This circuit can generate many unusual or complex waveforms. The output from this circuit is in the form of customized stepped waveforms. The discrete steps can be smoothed out somewhat by low-pass filtering.

Applications for this circuit include:

☐ Electronic music
☐ Sound effects generators
☐ Simulations of mathematical functions
☐ Imitating the unique signals or signatures emitted by natural phenomena such as the human heartbeat, nerve impulses, and earthquakes
☐ Specialized testing of electronic circuits

Operation of this circuit is fairly straightforward. A variable frequency clock generator continuously sends pulses to the counter. The binary output of the counter is decoded into 1-of-n outputs

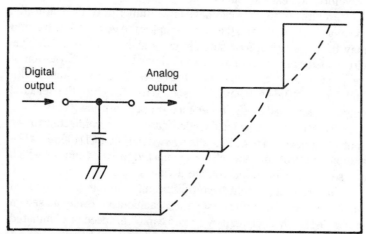

Fig. 9-10. A capacitor across the output smooths out the sharp corners of the waveform.

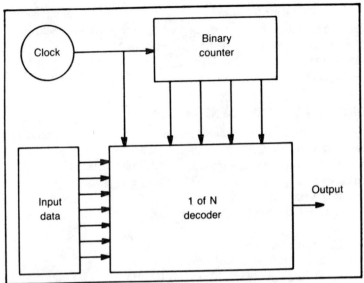

Fig. 9-11. This programmable function generator can produce many different waveshapes.

by a decoder stage. For each state of the counter, one and only one output from the decoder is active.

The decoder outputs are connected to individual switches. Each switch can apply a preselected voltage to a common OR-wired output. As the decoder sequentially actuates the switches, a stepped waveform appears at the output.

Circuits of this type can have any number of steps. Naturally, the more steps there are, the more complex the generated waveform may be. A practical four step circuit is shown in Fig. 9-12. This circuit is designed around the 7555 timer IC, a CMOS version of the popular 555. (See Chapter 6.) A CD4017 decade counter with built in 1-of-10 decoder is also used. With this chip, the selected output is high, all of the other nine outputs are low.

The four lowest-order decoded outputs are connected to the control inputs of each of four analog switches of a CD4066 IC. The analog inputs of each switch are connected to 10 k trimpots which are set up as adjustable voltage dividers.

The resulting output from this circuit is a four stage stepped waveform. Six clock pulses separate each output cycle, as shown in Fig. 9-13. This between-cycle gap can be reduced or eliminated by using the reset input of the CD4017 (pin #15). Simply connect one of the six unused decoder outputs to the reset input.

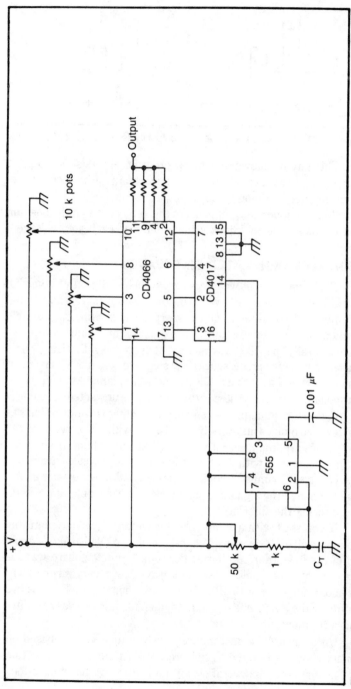

Fig. 9-12. The schematic for a practical four-step programmable function generator.

185

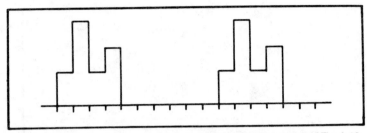

Fig. 9-13. Six clock pulses separate each output cycle in the circuit of Fig. 9-12.

This circuit allows you to preprogram any desired stepped waveform, without viewing the actual waveform on an oscilloscope. You only need to monitor each step voltage.

You can build the front panel of this project so that the position of the potentiometer knobs visually indicate each step voltage.

DIGITALLY GENERATED SINE WAVES

The most difficult waveform to synthesize digitally is the sine wave, because the sine wave is all slow, smooth curves, and digital circuits are best suited to quick, sharp corners. Still, it is possible to digitally synthesize a fair approximation of a sine wave.

Generally speaking, any method of digitally synthesizing a sine wave is a two-step process. The first step is to generate a convenient stepped waveform that consists of a fundamental and some harmonics. The second step is to filter out the unwanted harmonics.

For best results, pick a convenient starting waveform that has as few harmonics as possible to begin with. The weaker the harmonics are, the easier it will be to get rid of them. If you start with a waveform with relatively few and fairly weak harmonics, you can greatly simplify the filtering process. Moreover, this allows you to change the signal frequency over a reasonable range without altering the filtering.

If you start with a symmetrical waveform, you automatically eliminate all of the even harmonics. Ideally, you'd also like to avoid all of the low-order odd harmonics too. A simple square wave is not a very good choice. A square wave has a very strong third harmonic (down only 10 dB). The third harmonic's amplitude is two thirds of the amplitude of the fundamental. It is not easy to filter out a harmonic this strong.

Unfortunately almost any relatively simple system based on binary counters like the circuit presented in the previous section of this chapter has several strong low-order odd harmonics too.

186

The best approach for generating the starting waveform is to use a walking-ring or a Johnson counter. A suitable walking ring counter can be constructed out of type-D flip-flops or shift registers. The CD4018 D-type flip-flop IC is a good choice for 6, 8, or 10 step sine wave synthesis.

To build a walking ring counter from D-type flip-flops, simply connect the Q output of one stage to the D input of next stage. At last stage use the complementary (– Q) output to feed back to the D input of the first stage. Five stages give a ten step waveform. Normally, the sequence length is twice the number of stages.

In the example of five stages, the clocking sequence looks like this:

$$00000$$
$$10000$$
$$11000$$
$$11100$$
$$11110$$
$$11111$$
$$01111$$
$$00111$$
$$00011$$
$$00001$$
$$00000$$

The outputs, as illustrated in Fig. 9-14, are five phase-shifted square waves.

There is an inevitable compromise in the length of the counter. Longer counters have more parts, and are more expensive, but the output signal has higher and weaker odd harmonics.

As in the earlier digital waveform generator, the outputs are combined with resistors. Either a single small value summing resistor or the summing input of an op amp may be used. Skipping one counter stage in the summing makes the final sine wave automatically take twice as long on peaks and valleys. This gives a smoother and more natural sine wave.

Moderate precision is required for the summing resistances. It is not advisable to use 10 percent or 20 percent tolerance resistors, but the values are not overly critical. Generally, the nearest standard 5 percent or 1 percent resistor available will do just fine. Using out of tolerance resistors adds lower odd-order harmonics to the signal. Luckily, this problem need not be severe. For most variations

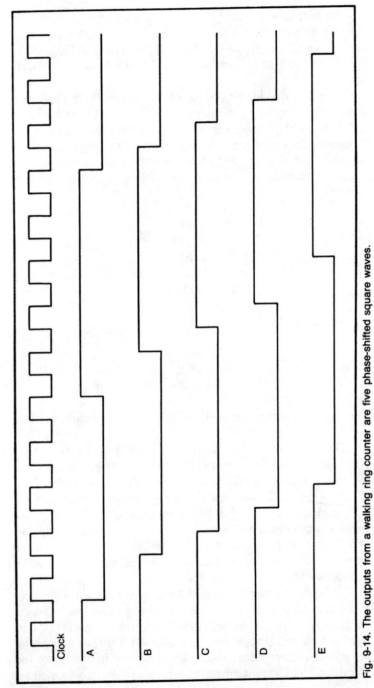

Fig. 9-14. The outputs from a walking ring counter are five phase-shifted square waves.

for 5 percent resistors, these added low-order harmonics are 40 dB below the fundamental, or lower. Typical resistance ratios for three, four, and five stage circuits are shown in Fig. 9-15.

The generated waveform certainly looks strange and choppy before filtering, but our goal is not a pretty waveform. The funny-looking waveform has virtually no low-order harmonics, and that is the important consideration here.

A ten-step walking ring counter with the proper resistances puts out a signal with no harmonics below the ninth, and even that harmonic is almost 20 dB down (1/10 amplitude) from the fundamental, even before filtering. A simple low-pass filter removes almost all of the harmonics, as shown in Fig. 9-16. For many applications, no filtering is needed at all, because the harmonic content is so high in frequency, and so low in amplitude that it is almost negligible.

The system clock frequency sets the generator's output frequency. The output frequency is one tenth of the clock frequency. As the clock frequency changes, so does the output frequency. The output frequency responds to changes in the clock frequency almost instantly because there are no time constraints or inductors in the circuit. Another helpful feature is that any sudden change in the clock frequency coherently changes the sine wave at the output, without any noticeable transients or jumps.

Any walking ring counter with more than two stages can get locked up on disallowed states. For example, for a three stage counter, the valid states are:

$$000$$
$$100$$
$$110$$
$$111$$
$$011$$
$$001$$

But the following are disallowed states:

$$101$$
$$010$$

If the counter somehow enters one of these two disallowed states, it loops between them endlessly. The circuit must be carefully designed to avoid such disallowed states. Fortunately, this

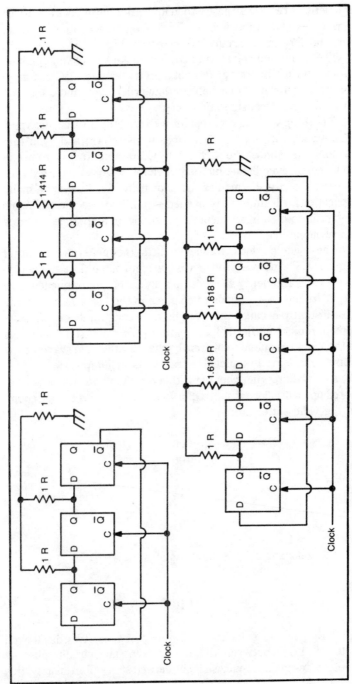

Fig. 9-15. Some typical resistance ratios for three, four, and five stage circuits.

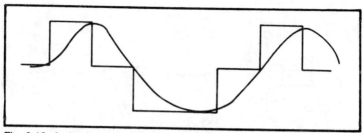

Fig. 9-16. A simple low-pass filter can remove almost all of the harmonics.

is done internally in the CD4018. Cascaded 4018s eliminate most, if not all, disallowed states. To forestall any problems, use a reset button or reset signal to force the circuit to start the sequence off on an allowed state (000).

Alternately, external logic gating can force the internal stages to 0 when the end stages are zero, or to all when the end stages are 1s.

A word of warning, however: A long reset pulse on a common reset line for all of the stages could permanently hang up the register. If you have only a common reset line for all stages, be sure to shorten the reset pulse.

The output signal from this type of circuit has some dc offset, which has to be eliminated before the sine wave can be used. The simplest method for dealing with the dc offset is to use a blocking capacitor in the output. Our sample circuit includes such a blocking capacitor.

MUSIC-MAKING CIRCUITS

Circuits that play music or produce sound effects have always been popular among electronics hobbyists. In recent years, electronic instruments have been used in almost every conceivable style of music.

Digital circuitry is surprisingly well suited to the production of musical sounds. Most commercially available music synthesizers around today are digital devices. The nature of digital signals make many effects easy that would be difficult, or even impossible using just analog techniques. Of course, the other side of the coin is just as valid. Some effects are best achieved with analog devices.

This section looks at several digital music-making circuits. Many of these signal generators could also be adapted for use in other applications.

Obviously, digital clock pulse generators are good sources for

191

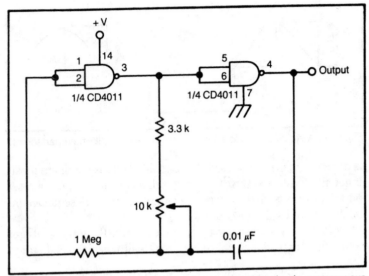

Fig. 9-17. Musical tones can be produced with this simple square-wave generator circuit.

harmonic-rich rectangle or square waves. The only special requirement for musical applications is that the output frequency must be in the audible range (approximately 40 Hz to 16 kHz for musical purposes).

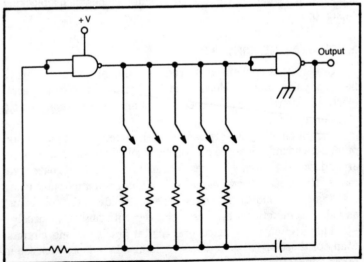

Fig. 9-18. Switch-selectable resistances convert the circuit of Fig. 9-17 into a simple monophonic organ.

As a starting point, let's use the simple square wave generator shown in Fig. 9-17. This circuit can be used for producing musical tones. It is not inherently different from some of the clock pulse generator circuits presented earlier in this chapter. The potentiometer (R3) can be used to move the output frequency up and down over most of the audible scale.

A simple monophonic organ can be created from this basic

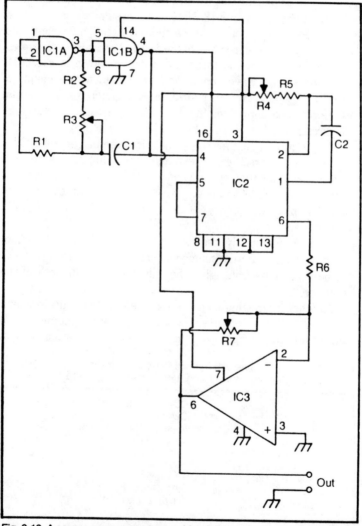

Fig. 9-19. A square wave generator combined with a couple of Schmitt triggers results in a staircase wave generator.

193

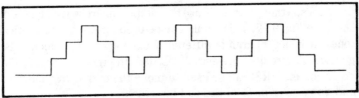

Fig. 9-20. This is the output waveform from the circuit of Fig. 9-19.

circuit, just be placing several switch selected resistances in parallel, as illustrated in Fig. 9-18. Note that pressing two or more keys simultaneously will not produce a chord. Instead, a frequency determined by the parallel values of the selected resistors is generated.

Another variation of this basic circuit is shown in Fig. 9-19. Here, the square wave generator is combined with a couple of Schmitt triggers to create a stair-case wave generator. The output waveform looks something like Fig. 9-20. The tones produced by this circuit will have a very bright, brassy sound.

A typical parts list for this project is given in Table 9-1. This circuit is quite versatile, and can generate a number of different waveshapes. Potentiometer R3 controls the number of steps in the output waveform, and thus the overall harmonic structure of the tone. The pitch (frequency) of the output signal is controlled by potentiometer R4.

Nothing is terribly critical in this circuit, so feel free to experiment with different component values. Some very odd effects can be achieved by changing the value(s) of one or both of the capacitors.

Another interesting complex tone generator circuit is shown in Fig. 9-21. Here a 555 timer is used to generate a rectangle wave signal, and four D flip-flops divide the frequency successively in

**Table 9-1. Typical Parts List for the
Staircase Wave Generator Circuit of Fig. 9-19.**

IC1	CD4011 quad NAND gate
IC2	CD4528 dual one shot
IC3	op amp (741, or similar)
R1	1 megohm resistor
R2	47 k resistor
R3, R4, R7	100 k potentiometer
R5, R6	10 k resistor
C1	0.01 μF capacitor *
C2	0.1 μF capacitor *
	* --- see text

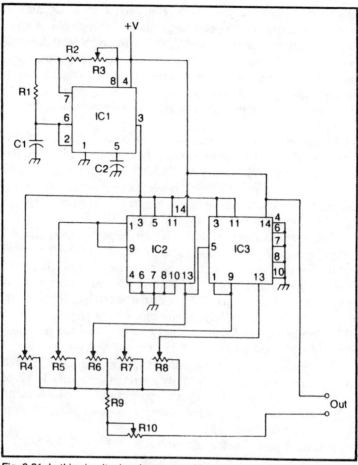

Fig. 9-21. In this circuit, signals separated by octaves can be blended in any combination.

half. This gives us five simultaneous signals with the following relationships:

$$F$$
$$F/2$$
$$F/4$$
$$F/8$$
$$F/16$$

F is the original frequency being generated by the 555 astable multivibrator. Each adjacent frequency is one octave lower than its immediate predecessor. The level of each of these signals can be independently set via potentiometers R4 through R8. A wide variety of combinations are possible, each with a somewhat different tonal quality. The ear does not hear these signals as separate tones; instead, they blend into a single complex tone. The effect is a very full and rich tone that is rather suggestive of an organ. (In fact, an organ actually combines multiple tone sources in a similar manner.)

Potentiometer R10 is a master volume control affecting all five of the signals together. The frequency of the main signal (F) is determined by the position of potentiometer R3. This control could be replaced by a series of switch-selectable resistors to form a rudimentary keyboard, allowing you to play simple tunes. A typical parts list for this project is given in Table 9-2.

A slightly different approach based on the same concept is used in the circuit of Fig. 9-22. Once again, the circuit starts with a simple rectangle wave, which is split into parts for separate manipulation to create new tonal colors. A 555 timer is once more used to generate the original signal. IC2 is a dual monostable multivibrator that delays the signal slightly, producing an intriguing out-of-phase effect. Potentiometer R5 determines how long this second signal is delayed, and R6 sets the width of the delayed pulse.

The original signal is combined with the delayed signal through an op amp mixer/amplifier (IC3). By altering the relative levels of the two signals and trying different settings of R5 and R6, many novel sounds can be generated. Commercial chorus effect units work on a similar principle.

A typical parts list for this project is given in Table 9-3.

**Table 9-2. Typical Parts List for the
Complex Tone Generator Circuit of Fig. 9-21.**

IC1	555 timer
IC2, IC3	CD4013 dual D flip-flop
R1	10 k resistor
R2	100 k resistor
R3	500 k potentiometer
R4 - R8	10 k potentiometer
R9	100 ohm resistor *
R10	1 k potentiometer *
C1, C2	0.01 μF capacitor
	* --- see text

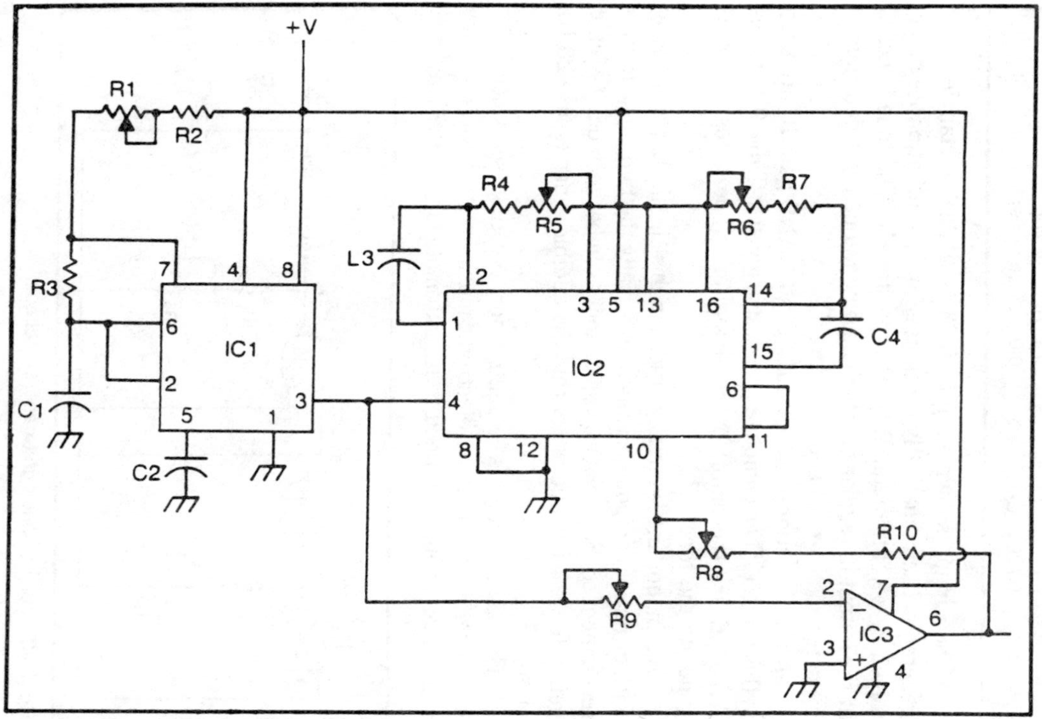

Fig. 9-22. A different approach to generating complex tones is used in this circuit.

IC1	555 timer
IC2	CD4528 dual one shot
IC3	op amp (741, or similar)
R1	100 k potentiometer
R2	10 k resistor
R3	3.3 k resistor
R4, R7	1 k resistor
R5, R6, R8, R9	10 k potentiometer
R10	22 k resistor
C1	0.1 μF capacitor
C2, C3, C4	0.01 μF capacitor

The circuit shown in Fig. 9-23 is a dual rectangle wave generator. It automatically turns itself on and off at a rate determined by potentiometer R3 and capacitor C1. The tone is heard at the output in regular bursts. The tone frequency is determined by potentiometer R6 and capacitor C2.

All four sections of a CD4011 quad NAND gate IC are used in this project. (The complete parts list is given in Table 9-4.) Gates A and B are the on/off burst generator, while gates C and D generate the tone.

Again, nothing is terribly crucial in this circuit. Experimenting with different component values, especially the two capacitors, is recommended. Some very complex tones can be created if the burst generator is set to operate within the audible range (above 20 Hz or so).

Digital circuitry is essential for creating sequencers. A sequencer is essentially an electronic music box that plays through a series of pre-programmed tones automatically. If the playback

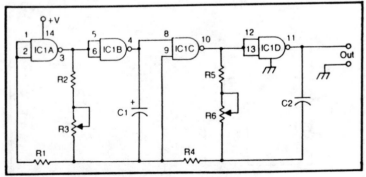

Fig. 9-23. A digital tone-burst generator circuit.

rate is very fast, the tones seem to blend into a single complex tone, so sequencers can also be employed as complex tone generators.

A basic four step sequencer circuit is shown in Fig. 9-24. The parts list for this project is given in Table 9-5.

The pitch of each of the four tones is set by potentiometer R6, R9, R12, or R15. The 555 timer circuit (IC) causes the output to step repeatedly through all four tones at a rate determined by potentiometer R2. For other effects, try different values for the timing capacitor (C1).

A more advanced sequencer circuit is shown in Fig. 9-25. The parts list for this project is given in Table 9-6.

This sequencer has ten steps, each individually set by potentiometers R5 through R14. The voltage passing through each potentiometer is used to drive the VCO circuit built around a 555 timer (IC3).

Potentiometer R15 is a master pitch control. The pitch range can be adjusted by changing the value of capacitor C2. Potentiometer R18 is a master volume control.

Unijunction transistor Q1, and its related components, controls the step rate for the circuit. The step rate is determined by the values of potentiometer R2 and capacitor C1. For a sequencer with distinct, separate tonal steps, try a capacitor between about 2 μF to 10 μF. If you'd rather use the circuit as a complex tone generator, C1's value should be made smaller—a 0.1 μF disc capacitor is suitable. There is plenty of room for experimentation in this circuit.

Many other digital sequencer circuits are also possible, but there isn't enough space to present them here.

A sequencer plays the same tones over and over in a continuous pattern, unless the control settings are changed. It is also possible to design digital circuits that create their own tunes. These circuits will randomly (or pseudo-randomly) select the tones to be sounded. The effects are sometimes quite fascinating. Occasionally a snatch of melody may be heard, but for the most part, the results sound totally random. Simple composing circuits have no musical taste or judgement at all.

The circuit shown in Fig. 9-26 produces a random series of tones, which may or may not correspond to a traditional musical scale. Potentiometer R2 determines the rate at which the tones change frequency. Potentiometer R19 controls the overall pitch range. Changing the position of rotary switch S1 alters the pattern noticeably. A suggested parts list for this project is given in Table 9-7.

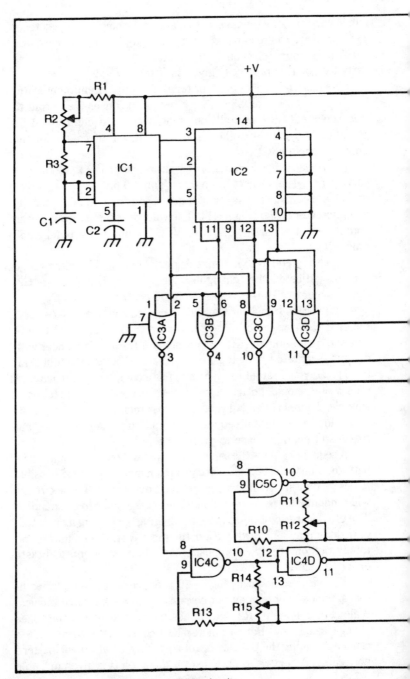

Fig. 9-24. A four-step digital sequencer circuit.

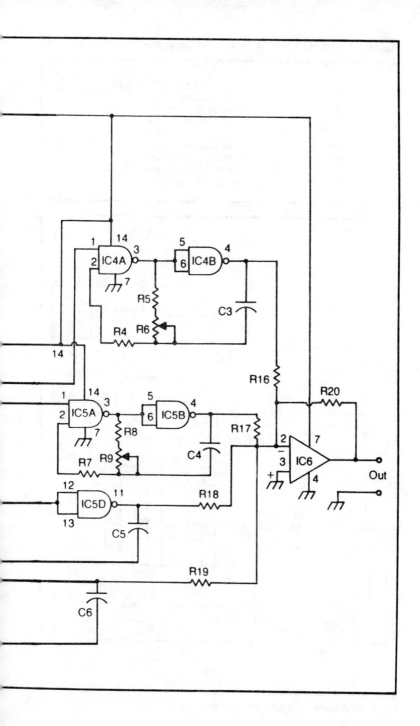

Table 9-4. Parts List for the Tone-Burst Generator Circuit of Fig. 9-23.

IC1	CD4011 quad NAND gate
R1	10 megohm resistor
R2	470 k resistor
R3	500 k potentiometer
R4	1 megohm resistor
R5	47 k resistor
R6	100 k potentiometer
C1	0.47 µF capacitor
C2	0.01 µF capacitor

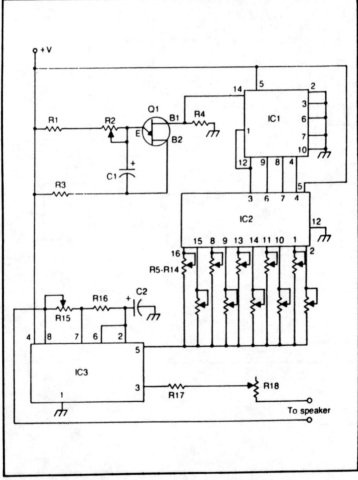

Fig. 9-25. A more advanced ten-step sequencer circuit.

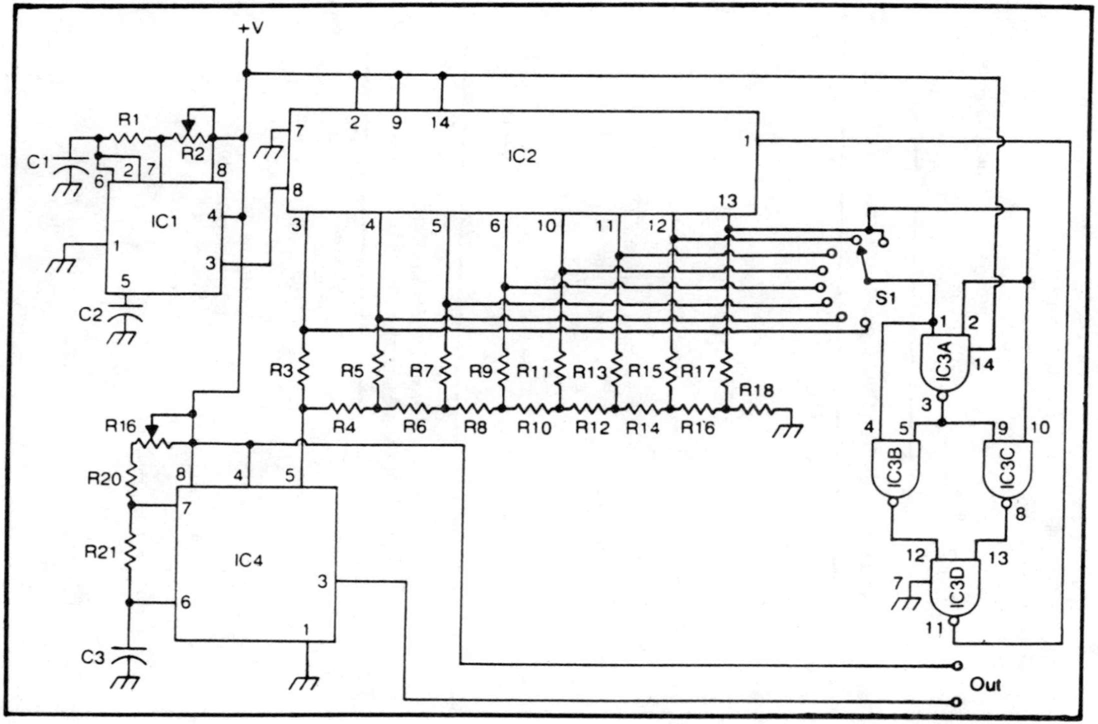

Fig. 9-26. This circuit generates a series of randomly selected tones.

Table 9-5. Parts List for the Four-Step Digital Sequencer Circuit of Fig. 9-24.

IC1	555 timer
IC2	CD4013 dual-D flip-flop
IC3	CD4001 quad NOR gate
IC4, IC5	CD4011 quad NAND gate
IC6	op amp (741. or similar)
R1	2.2 k resistor
R2, R6, R9, R12, R15	100 k potentiometer
R3	33 k resistor
R4, R7, R10, R13	1 megohm resistor
R5, R8, R11, R14	47 k resistor
R16 - R19	10 k resistor
R20	22 k resistor
C1	10 μF 35 volt electrolytic capacitor
C2 - C6	0.01 μF disc capacitor

Table 9-6. Parts List for the Ten-Step Digital Sequencer Circuit of Fig. 9-25.

IC1	7490
IC2	7441
IC3	555
Q1	UJT (2N4891. or similar)
R1	390 k resistor
R2	500 k potentiometer
R3	1 k resistor
R4, R17	100 ohm resistor
R5 - R14, R18	1 k potentiometer
R15	50 k potentiometer
R16	2.2 k resistor
C1	see text
C2	0.22 μF capacitor (see text)

**Table 9-7. Parts List for the Digital
Random Tone Generator Circuit of Fig. 9-26.**

IC1, IC4	555 timer
IC2	74164 8 bit shift register
IC3	7400 quad NAND gate
R1, R20	2.2 k resistor
R2, R19	100 k potentiometer
R3, R5, R7, R9, R11, R13, R15, R17, R18, R21	3 3 k resistor
R4, R6, R8, R10, R12, R14. R16	6 8 k resistor
C1, C3	0 1 μF capacitor
C2	0 01 μF capacitor
S1	1-pole. 8-throw rotary switch

Dedicated Signal
Generator ICs

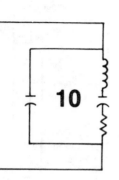

10

$\mathbf{I}$N THE LAST DECADE OR SO, MORE AND MORE ELECTRONIC
functions are being performed by specially designed integrated
circuits. Since oscillators and signal generators are such an
important part of so many electronics systems, it only stands to
reason that a number of signal generator ICs would be available.

So many signal generator ICs have been created that there is
no way to cover them all. This chapter considers just a few
representative examples.

THE XR-2206 FUNCTION GENERATOR

One popular signal generator IC is the XR-2206 function
generator IC, originally manufactured by Exar Integrated Systems,
Inc., and is now available from many distributers.

A functional block diagram of the XR-2206 is shown in Fig.
10-1. Housed in a standard 16 pin DIP, this powerful chip generates
high quality sine waves, square waves, triangle waves, sawtooth
waves and pulse waves at frequencies from a fraction of a hertz
to several kilohertz, with a minimum of external circuitry. The
output frequency can be swept over a 2000:1 range, using just a
single control-voltage or variable resistance.

The XR-2206 has facilities for AM (amplitude modulation), FM
(frequency modulation), PSK (phase shift keying), or FSK
(frequency shift keying) operations. This device is also very flexible
when it comes to power supplies. It can be powered from either

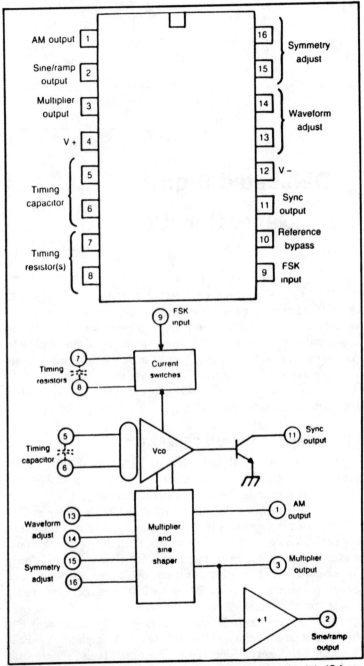

Fig. 10-1. The XR2206 is a high quality function generator circuit in IC form.

a single supply anywhere between +10 and +26 volts, or a split voltage supply in the range of ±5 to ±13 volts.

The XR-2206 can generate very pure sine waves. The THD is typically 2.5 percent, even without adjustment. The THD can be further reduced to about 0.5 percent with external trimmer controls. The typical maximum amplitude of the output sine wave is about 2 volts. The output impedance is a standard 600 ohms.

At the heart of the XR-2206 IC is a VCO that is driven by a pair of current switches. The VCO's main timing capacitor is externally wired between pins 5 and 6. This capacitor should have a value from 1000 pF to 100 μF. Similarly, the main timing resistor is externally connected between the negative supply voltage (V $\neg$) and pin #7 or #8. This resistance should be between 1 k and 2 megohms, but for optimum thermal stability and minimum sine wave distortion, R_t should be between 4 k and 200 k.

These two components, R_t (timing resistor) and C_t (timing capacitor), directly determine the output frequency, according to this simple formula:

$$F = 1/(R_t \times C_t)$$

The timing resistor can be connected to either pin #7 or #8, or two different timing resistors can be connected to these two pins for FSK operation.

Either pin #7 or #8 can be selected by applying a suitable voltage to the FSK input terminal (pin #9). If pin #9 is either open-circuited or connected to a bias voltage less than 2 volts, then the pin #7 resistor is selected. On the other hand, if pin #9 is biased below 1 volt, or grounded, then pin #8 is selected.

This FSK facility enables the output signal to be switched alternately between two independently adjustable frequencies. This can be used to produce a warble signal, or to encode digital data.

The VCO generates two basic waveforms simultaneously. One is a linear ramp which is fed to an internal multiplier and sine shaper. The other waveform is a rectangle wave which appears on pin #11 via a built-in buffer.

In the VCO, the timing capacitor (C_t) charges linearly through the timing resistor (R_t) to produce an internal rising ramp waveform. At the same time, the voltage appearing on pin #11 switches sharply from the low to the high state.

When the ramp exceeds a predetermined threshold voltage, the rectangle signal switches sharply back to low, and C_t starts charging in the reverse direction via R_t to produce a falling ramp until second threshold reached. Then the circuit switches back to start of pattern.

If the same timing resistor is used to control both charging cycles of C_t (no FSK), symmetrical triangle and square waves will be produced by the XR-2206. On the other hand, if the rectangle wave output at pin #11 is connected to the FSK input (pin #9), then different timing resistances can be used for the two halves of the cycle. This permits the generation of non-symmetrical ramp and rectangle/pulse waves.

The ramp signal from the VCO is fed to the multiplier and sine-shaper circuits, which act like a gain-controlled differential amplifier. This provides a high impedance output at pin #3 and a 600 ohm buffered output at pin #2. With pins #13 and #14 left open, a ramp waveform appears at pins #2 and #3. Alternatively, with a resistance of a few hundred ohms connected between pins #13 and #14, the circuit exponentially cuts off the positive and negative peaks of the ramp signal from the VCO. This creates a sine wave at pins #2 and #3. With suitable adjustment, the sine wave distortion can be reduced to a mere 0.5 percent.

The gain and output phase of the multiplier can be varied by applying a bias or signal voltage to pin #1. The output is linearly controlled by variations above and below a level equal to one-half the supply voltage. The output is zero when the pin #1 voltage equals one-half the supply voltage. The output rises as the pin #1 voltage increases over one-half the supply voltage. Of course, the output amplitude falls as the pin #1 voltage is decreased below one-half supply voltage. In this case, the phase is reversed. This characteristic of the XR-2206 can be used to amplitude modulate (AM) or phase shift key (PSK) the output signals at pins #2 and #3.

The input signal to the buffer (and therefore the output signal at pin #2) can be varied by connecting a voltage divider between pin #3 and ground. This technique adds the capability of simple gain control of the output, or it can be used for keying or pulsing the output signal at pin #2.

In most applications, pin #3 will be biased halfway between the positive and negative supply voltages. In split supply circuits, this means the output signal swings about the 0 volt (common) line.

Now let's take a look at a few circuits using the XR-2206 function generator IC.

A high quality sine wave circuit is shown in Fig. 10-2. In this circuit, the timing resistance is provided by the series combination

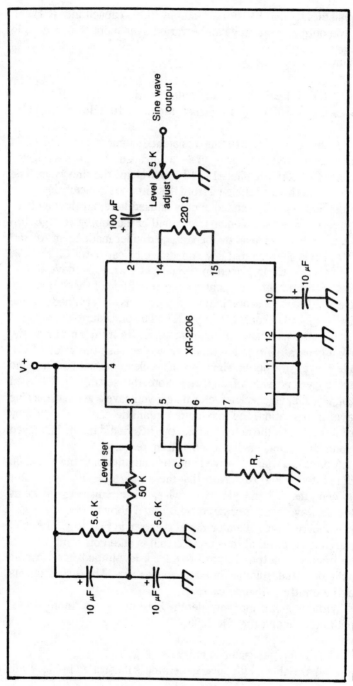

Fig. 10-2. This circuit causes the XR2206 to generate reasonably pure sine waves.

209

of resistors R1 and R2. For any single timing capacitance (C1) value, the output frequency can be varied over more than a decade range.

Some suggested values for C1 are:

☐ C1 = 1 μF—frequency range = 10 Hz to 100 Hz
☐ C1 = 1000 pF—frequency range = 10 kHz to 100 kHz

In this circuit the timing resistance connected to pin #7 is automatically selected since pin #9 is unbiased. A 220 ohm resistor is connected between pins #13 and #14 to shape the sine wave. The distortion in the output signal from this circuit is typically less than 2.5 percent. A single ended supply is used here, so the dc offset voltage at the output is equal to one-half of the supply voltage. Pin #3 is biased at that level by the voltage divider made up of R6 and R7, which is shunted to a low impedance by capacitor C3 and C4.

Capacitor C5 is placed in the output path to remove the dc offset. Potentiometer R5 controls the amplitude of the output sine wave. The circuit's maximum amplitude is determined by the LEVEL PRESET control (trimpot R3). The procedure for adjusting this control is as follows. First, disconnect R4 from pin #13, so the IC will generate a triangle wave. Now, decrease the value of R3, while viewing the output signal on an oscilloscope, until the triangle wave shows no sign of clipping. Note the setting of R3, then reconnect R4 and check to determine if you have a good, clean sine shape. In operation, the maximum amplitude can be reduced by setting R3 below the noted setting, but R3 should not be increased beyond this point, or distortion will increase.

A practical triangle wave generator circuit using the XR-2206 is illustrated in Fig. 10-3. Note that there is no sine shaping resistor between pins #13 and #14. Otherwise, this circuit is the same as the sine wave generator circuit discussed above.

A square wave generator circuit is shown in Fig. 10-4. The chief difference here is that the output signal is taken off from pin #11. The transistor output circuit provides a low-impedance variable amplitude output suitable for many applications. These components may be omitted in some cases.

Without going into any depth, here are a few more useful circuits employing the XR-2206.

☐ A ramp generator is shown in Fig. 10-5.
☐ A variable width pulse generator is illustrated in Fig. 10-6.

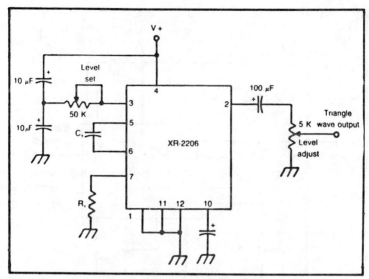

Fig. 10-3. A triangle wave generator can be created simply by deleting the sine shaping resistor between pins #13 and #14.

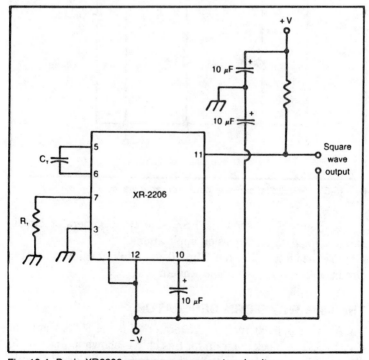

Fig. 10-4. Basic XR2206 square wave generator circuit.

211

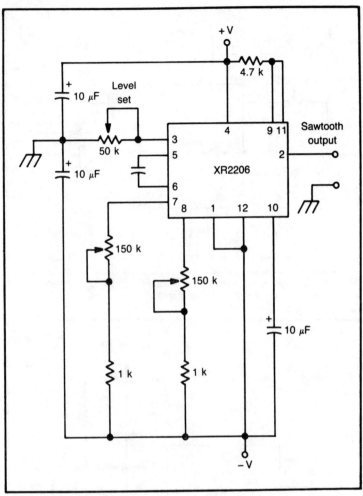

Fig. 10-5. The XR2206 can also generate ramp waves.

☐ Figure 10-7 shows a FSK sine wave generator circuit suitable for data transmission applications.

☐ The circuit shown in Fig. 10-8 is a full function generator circuit with switch selectable waveforms.

THE 8038 WAVEFORM GENERATOR

Another popular function generator IC is the 8038, shown in Fig. 10-9. The block diagram for this chip is shown in Fig. 10-10. The 8038's internal circuitry includes two externally adjustable

212

constant-current sources, a pair of comparators, a flip-flop, buffer amplifiers, and sine converter, all in a standard 14-pin DIP housing.

Sine, square, triangle, sawtooth and pulse waveforms can be generated by the 8038 with a frequency range from less than 0.001 Hz to over 1.0 MHz. The output frequency is independent of the supply voltage and generally depends only on the values of the external timing resistor and capacitor.

The 8038 can be either frequency modulated, or swept over a wide range simply by applying an appropriate control voltage to pin #8.

The 8038 is extremely stable. The maximum rated frequency drift for the 8038 is merely 50 ppm/degree C. This chip also offers low distortion. It is rated for a typical distortion level of 1.0 percent or less. The linearity rating is also quite impressive. According to the manufacturer's specification sheet, the linearity is 0.1 percent or better.

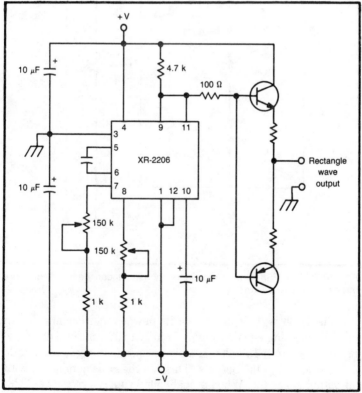

Fig. 10-6. A variable width rectangle wave generator circuit using the XR2206.

213

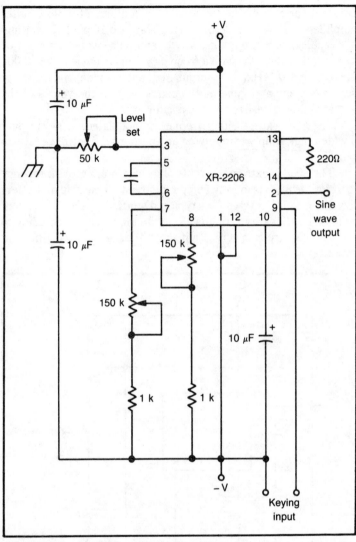

Fig. 10-7. This FSK sine wave generator circuit can be used for data transmission applications.

The 8038 is very flexible in its power requirements. It can operate on a single-ended supply from 10 to 30 volts or a dual supply from ±5 to ±15 volts. If a single ended supply is used, a dc offset is added to the outputs. This can easily be eliminated with an output capacitor. When a dual-ended supply drives the 8038, all of the outputs are centered around 0.

214

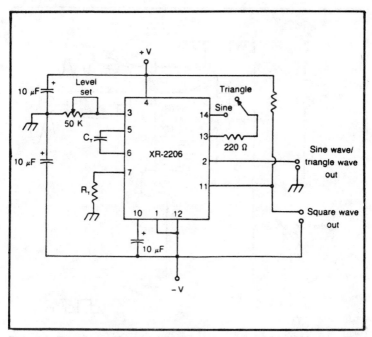

Fig. 10-8. This circuit uses the XR2206 as the heart of a complete function generator.

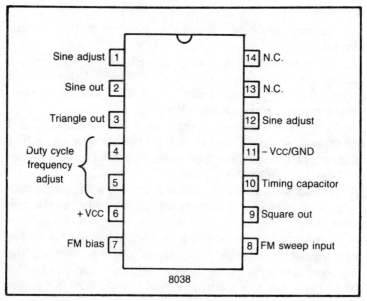

Fig. 10-9. Another popular function generator IC is the 8038.

215

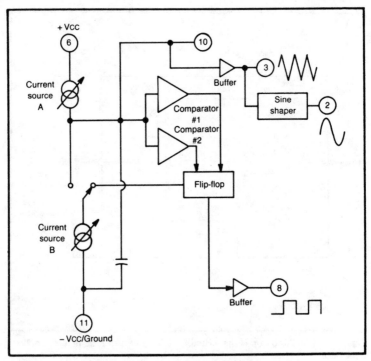

Fig. 10-10. Block diagram of the 8038's internal circuitry.

The rectangle output is suitable for driving TTL devices directly.

The 8038's output frequency depends on the value of the external timing capacitor between pin #10 and – VCC (or circuit ground) and the values of the two external timing resistors connecting pins #4 and #5 to + VCC.

The symmetry of the waveforms varies with the duty cycle and this depends on the relative values of the two timing resistors. The 8038 offers a wide range of duty cycles. The duty cycle can be varied from 2 percent to 98 percent.

Symmetrical waveforms are obtained with a 50 percent duty cycle. The symmetrical outputs are triangle, sine, and square waves. As the duty cycle is increased or decreased, the triangle wave begins to become more of a sawtooth wave, and the square wave becomes a rectangle wave, approaching a pulse wave. The sine wave also becomes highly distorted, since the internal sine shaper circuitry requires a symmetrical triangle wave for proper shaping action.

216

A versatile circuit designed around the 8038 is shown in Fig. 10-11. By adjusting the two potentiometers, the operator has full control over both the frequency and waveform symmetry. A 50 percent duty cycle (symmetrical waveforms) is obtained when the resistors have equal values. That is;

$$R_a = R_b$$

The circuit shown in Fig. 10-12 permits a small variation of the duty cycle on either side of the 50 percent point while holding the output frequency constant.

By contrast, the circuit of Fig. 10-13 does not permit adjustment of the duty cycle. The single potentiometer is used to control the

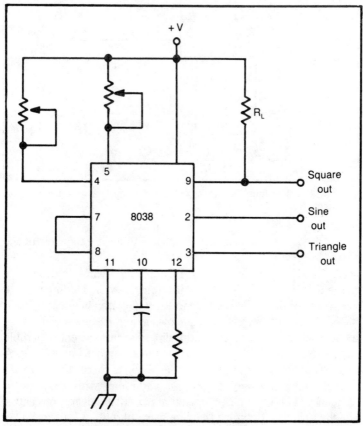

Fig. 10-11. In this 8038 function generator, both the frequency and the waveform symmetry are manually variable.

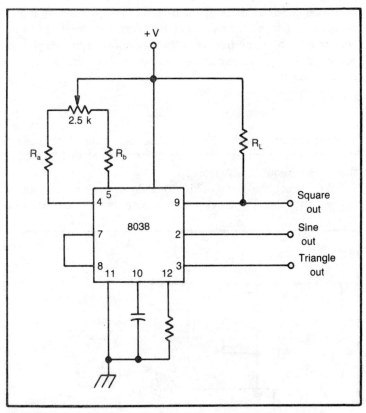

Fig. 10-12. This circuit has an adjustable duty cycle and a fixed output frequency.

output frequency. This is the simplest and least expensive of the three designs shown here.

A 1000:1 range is achieved by applying a variable dc control to the IC's FM sweep input terminal (pin #8) while holding voltage across the timing resistors Ra and Rb at a relatively low level with a IN457 series diode. The circuit shown in Fig. 10-14 is a wide range audio oscillator. The output of this circuit covers the entire audible range—from 20 Hz to 20 kHz, all without any band-switching. A large trimpot (typically about 15 megohms) is connected to pin #5 to help minimize any duty-cycle variations with changes in frequency. The 100 k potentiometer at pin #12 is a distortion control which is used to optimize the sine wave output. A pair of 8038s can be cascaded, with one functioning as a sweep signal source for the second.

VCO ICS

A number of dedicated VCO circuits in IC form have been put on the market over the last few years. Several are designed specifically for electronic music systems, but these devices could be put to work in other applications too.

One such device is the CEM3340, which is manufactured by Curtis electronics. A practical VCO circuit using the CEM3340 is shown in Fig. 10-15. A typical parts list for this circuit is given in Table 10-1.

Solid State Micro Technology is another manufacturer of VCO ICs. Figure 10-16 shows a circuit using their SSM2030. Table 10-2 shows a typical parts list. Resistor R1 deserves some special attention here. The function of this resistor is to compensate for changes in temperature and cancel out oscillator drift. The value of this resistor is critical. For maximum precision, add a 121 ohm

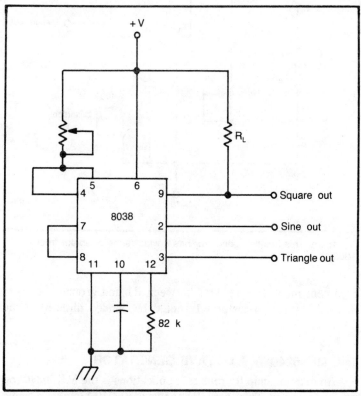

Fig. 10-13. This simple function generator has a variable output frequency, but the waveform symmetry (duty cycle) is fixed.

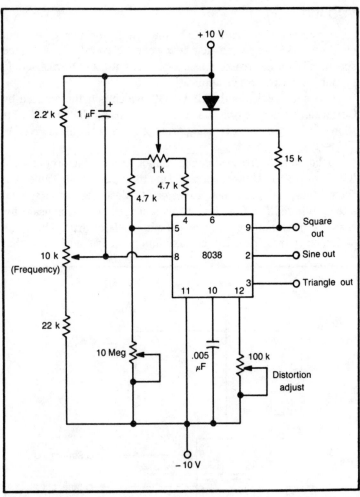

Fig. 10-14. This function generator has a wide range of output frequencies (1000:1).

1 percent metal film resistor between R1 and ground. For best thermal stability, resistor R1 should be bonded directly to the SSM2030.

THE MK50240 TOP OCTAVE GENERATOR

An exciting chip for musical applications is the MK50240 top octave generator. This 16 pin IC, shown in Fig. 10-17, takes a single input frequency and divides it by various values to produce a full

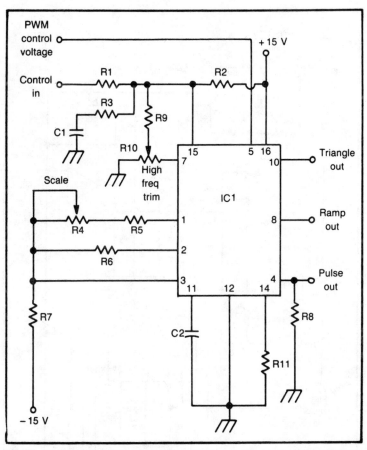

Fig. 10-15. The CEM3340 is a dedicated VCO IC designed for use in electronic music applications.

Table 10-1. Typical Parts List for the CEM3340 VCO Circuit of Fig. 10-15.

IC1	CEM3340 VCO IC
C1	0.01 μF capacitor
C2	0.001 μF capacitor
R1	100 k resistor
R2	360 k resistor
R3	470 ohm resistor
R4	5 k trimpot
R5	27 k resistor
R6	5.6 k resistor
R7	820 ohm resistor
R8	10 k resistor
R9	1 megohm resistor
R10	10 k trimpot
R11	1.8 k resistor

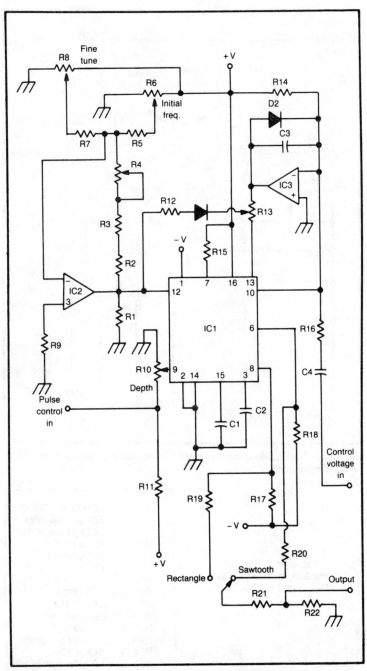

Fig. 10-16. Another dedicated VCO IC is the SSM2030.

Table 10-2. Typical Parts List for the SSM2030 VCO Circuit of Fig. 10-16.

IC1	SSM2030 VCO IC
IC2, IC3	high quality op amp
D1, D2	1N914 diode
C1, C2	1000 pF capacitor
C3	100 pF capacitor
C4	0.1 μF capacitor
R1	1 k resistor (see text)
R2	56 k resistor
R3	91 k resistor
R4	25 k trimpot
R5	4.7 megohm resistor
R6, R8, R10	100 k trimpot
R7	270 k resistor
R9	47 k resistor
R11, R17, R18	22 k resistor
R12	470 k resistor
R13	10 k trimpot
R14	2.2 megohm resistor
R15	2.2 k resistor
R16	1.5 megohm resistor
R19, R20	270 k resistor
R21	39 k resistor
R22	68 k resistor

octave in an equally tempered scale. The division factors are as follows:

PIN #	DIVISOR
15	239
14	253
13	268
12	284
11	301
10	319
9	338
8	358
7	379
6	402
5	426
4	451
16	478

Thirteen of the pins on this chip are taken up by the outputs. Of the three remaining pins, two are used for power supply

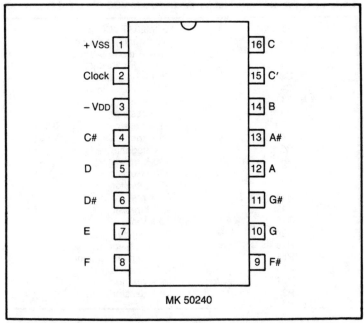

Fig. 10-17. The MK50240 top octave generator is useful for creating polyphonic musical instruments.

connections, and the third is the input pin. This all suggests that the MK50240 is very easy to use. The basic circuit is shown in Fig. 10-18. Two NAND gates are wired as inverters to generate the clock pulses. To produce musical tones, the clock should have a high frequency (nominally about 2 MHz). The clock capacitor should have a value from 15 pF to 500 pF.

The MK50240 can also be used as a pseudo-random voltage source, just by slowing down the input clock pulses. This can be done by using a larger value for the clock capacitor (1 μF to 50 μF).

The outputs from the MK50240 top octave generator IC are square waves.

SOUND EFFECTS GENERATORS

A number of available ICs are called "synthesizers on a chip." They are essentially a complete sound synthesizer system contained in a single IC package. They are comprised of sub-circuits like VCOs, VCFs (voltage-controlled filters), VCAs (voltage-controlled amplifiers), envelope generators, and noise generators. A handful of external resistors and capacitors, along with some switches (or

224

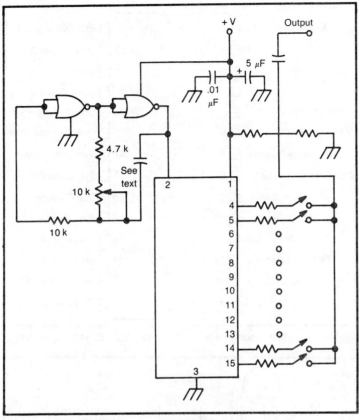

Fig. 10-18. Basic circuit for the MK50240 top octave generator.

hard-wired connections) program the specific parameters of the sound to be generated.

These devices tend to be more suited to creating sound effects, rather than actual music. Their most common applications are in video games and related products.

The first important sound effect generator IC was the SN76477 from Texas Instruments. This 28 pin device is illustrated in Fig. 10-19. A block diagram of its internal circuitry is shown in Fig. 10-20.

The SN76477 can be powered by anything from +7.5 to +9 volts dc. It contains a +5 volt regulator that can supply up to 10 mA at pin #15. Alternately, the chip can be operated by applying a regulated +5 volts to pin #15. In either case, pin #2 is the ground connection.

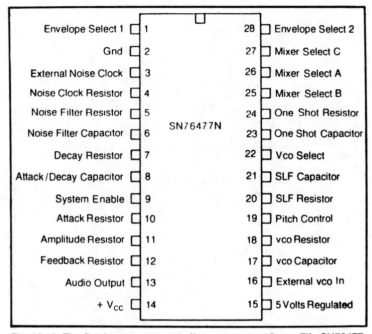

Fig. 10-19. The first important sound effects generator IC was TI's SN76477.

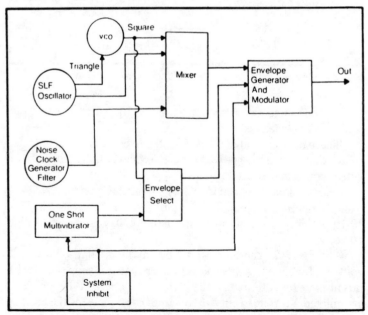

Fig. 10-20. Simplified block diagram for the SN76477 sound effects generator.

A small audio amplifier is built into the IC, but further amplification is generally needed to bring the signal level up to a useful level. The manufacturer suggests the simple two-transistor amplifier shown in Fig. 10-21. To use the SN76477 to drive an external amplifier use the connections shown in Fig. 10-22.

The SN76488 is an improved version of the SN76477. The two devices are similar, but the SN76488 has a more powerful built-in output amplifier stage.

Pin #9 is the master enable switch for the IC. If this pin is grounded, the IC is allowed to function. Feeding + 5 volts to pin #9 disables the chip. The other 21 pins (excluding the master enable switch, and the power supply related pins) are used to program desired sounds. Either resistors, capacitors, variable voltage, or switches are connected to these pins:

Pin	Component Type	Range	Function Section
20	R	7.5 k to 1 M	Super Low Frequency
21	C	500 pF to 100 μF	Oscillator
18	R	7.5 k to 1 M	Voltage-Controlled
17	C	100 pF to 1 μF	Oscillator
19	V	(normally + 5 V)—duty cycle	
22	S	+ 5 V = SLF O = pin 16	
16	V	High voltage = Low frequency	
4	R	switch (43 k)	Noise
5	R	7.5 k to 1 M	
6	C	150 pF to 0.01μF	
25	S		Mixer
26	S		
27	S		
23	C	0.1 to 50 μF	One shot
24	R	7.5 k to 1 meg	
1			Envelope
28			
7	R	7.5 k to 1 M	Decay
8	C	.01 to 10 μF	Timing
10	R	7.5 k to 1 M	Attack

$$C = \text{Capacitor}$$
$$R = \text{Resistor}$$
$$S = \text{Switch}$$
$$V = \text{Control Voltage}$$

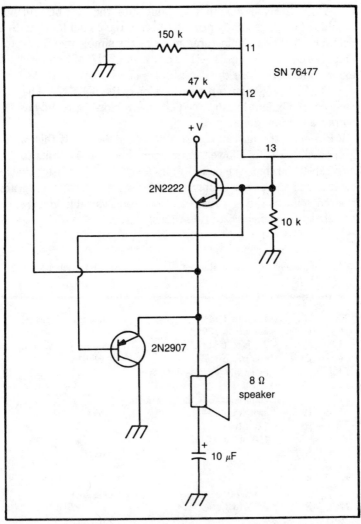

Fig. 10-21. This simple two-transistor amplifier circuit can be used to boost the output from the SN76477.

Each of the resistors and capacitors are wired between the indicated pin and ground. All switches select between +5 volts and ground (0 volts).

The section labelled SLF is a Super Low Frequency oscillator. It is used to provide ac control signals to other portions of the SN76477 (specifically the VCO and/or the mixer). The SLF's nominal range is from 0.1 Hz to 30 Hz, but this oscillator can be forced to operate at a much higher frequency if needed.

The basic tonal output is originally supplied by the VCO stage. This section is not too different from the VCO circuits discussed back in Chapter 7. The basic frequency of the VCO is determined by the resistance at pin #18 and the capacitance at pin #17. The VCO frequency can also be affected by either the output voltage from the SLF or by an external voltage applied to pin #16. The choice between the SLF or the external input is made at pin #22.

A voltage applied to pin #19 controls the duty cycle of VCO's output waveform. Normally, pin #19 is shorted to pin #15 for +5 volts (50 percent duty cycle).

The SN76477's noise source is controlled by pin #4. Leaving this pin unconnected turns the noise source off, while shorting pin #4 to ground through a 43 k resistor turns the noise source on. If you prefer, you can feed in an external noise source at pin #3.

The mixer stage offers eight binary switching options (from 000 to 111). A 0 represents a grounded pin (0 volts), while a 1 represents +5 volts dc at the indicated pin.

Each option results in a different combination of active elements in the system reaching the output:

$$000 = VCO$$
$$001 = SLF$$
$$010 = Noise$$

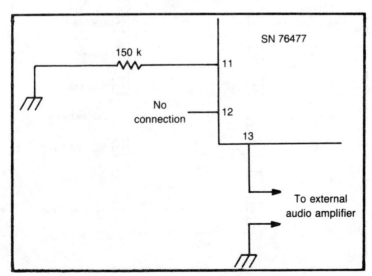

Fig. 10-22. The SN76477 can drive an external amplifier.

011	=	VCO and Noise
100	=	SLF and Noise
101	=	SLF, VCO and Noise
110	=	SLF and VCO
111	=	inhibit all

The SN76477 is such a complex and versatile device, an entire book could be written on just this single IC; however, there isn't space to go into detail here.

Despite the complexity of the SN76477, it is surprisingly easy to use. Just approach each stage (for example, the VCO, the SLF, etc.) individually. The chip is supplied with a data sheet that explains how to choose each of the external component values.

Another sound effects generator IC is the slightly simpler SN94281, shown in Fig. 10-23. It contains an on-chip 125 mW output amplifier stage. The SN94281 functions in basically the same manner as the SN76477.

The AY-3-8910, shown in Fig. 10-24, is a programmable sound effects generator. It is designed for computer controlled applications. Eight-bit digital values are stored in each of the chip's

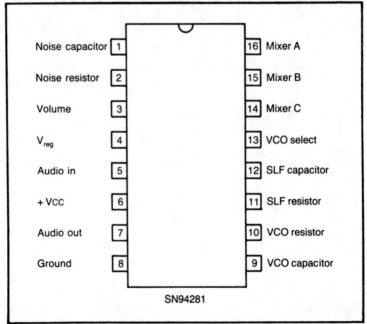

Fig. 10-23. The SN94281 is a somewhat simpler sound effects generator IC.

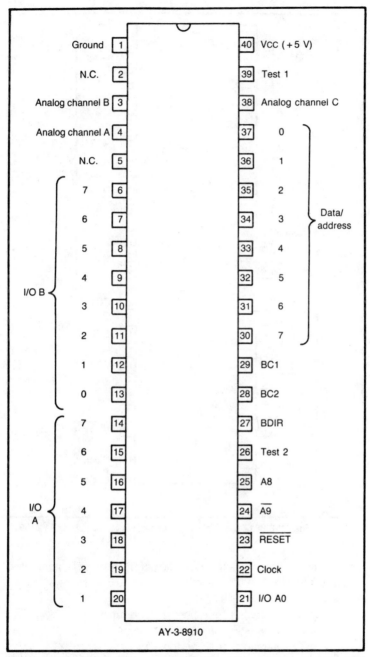

Fig. 10-24. The AY-3-8910 Programmable Sound Generator is a very powerful computer peripheral.

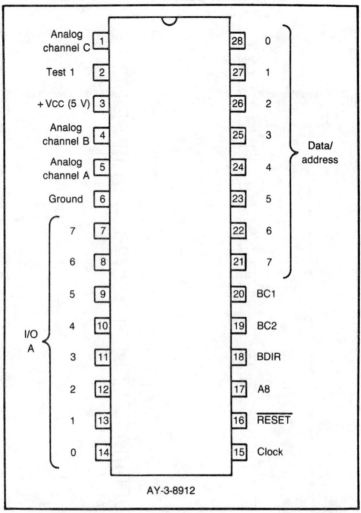

Fig. 10-25. The AY-3-8912 is a slightly stripped-down version of the AY-3-8910 PSG.

sixteen internal registers to define the parameters of the generated sounds. The AY-3-890's internal registers are as follows:

R00 Channel A tone period—fine tune
R01 Channel A tone period—coarse tune
R02 Channel B tone period—fine tune
R03 Channel B tone period—coarse tune
R04 Channel C tone period—fine tune

R05　Channel C tone period—coarse tune
R06　Noise period
R07　Enable
R10　Channel A amplitude
R11　Channel B amplitude
R12　Channel C amplitude
R13　Envelope period—fine tune
R14　Envelope period—coarse tune
R15　Envelope shape/cycle
R16　I/O Port A data store
R17　I/O Port B data store

The AY-3-8910 has three independently controllable tone sources, along with a noise source. Some very complex sounds, and even simple music, can be generated by this device.

A smaller version of the AY-3-8910 is the AY-3-8912, which is shown in Fig. 10-25. The main difference between these two devices is that the AY-3-8912 has just one I/O port, while the AY-3-8910 has two. This may or may not be significant, depending on the specific system being used.

Index

Index

239

Other Bestsellers From TAB

Other Bestsellers From TAB